studysync®

Reading & Writing Companion

No Risk, No Reward

Why do we take chances?

::studysync®

studysync.com

Send all inquiries to:
BookheadEd Learning, LLC
610 Daniel Young Drive
Sonoma, CA 95476

ISBN 978-1-94-469587-3

4 5 6 LMN 24 23 22 21 20

B

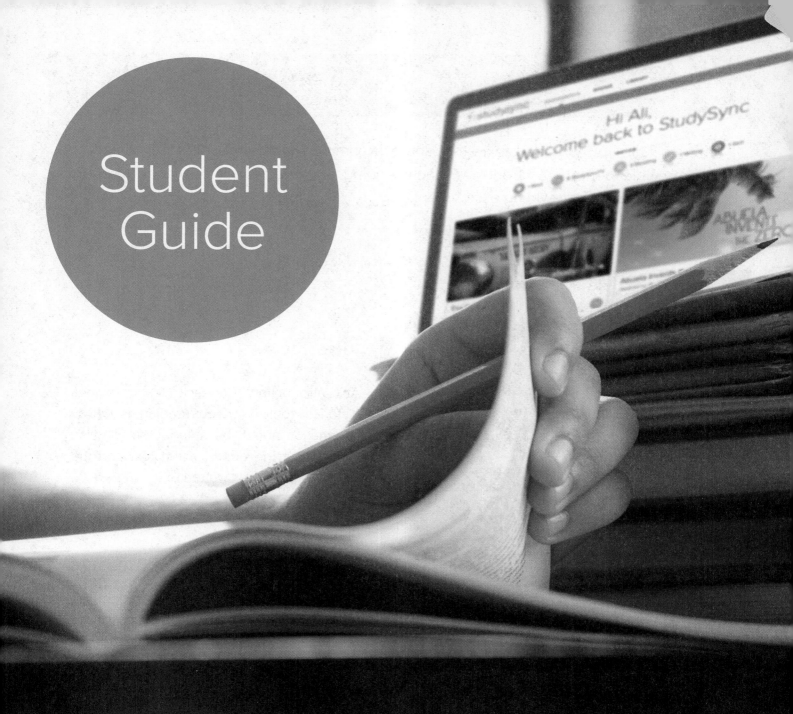

Student Guide

Getting Started

Welcome to the StudySync Reading & Writing Companion! In this book, you will find a collection of readings based on the theme of the unit you are studying. As you work through the readings, you will be asked to answer questions and perform a variety of tasks designed to help you closely analyze and understand each text selection. Read on for an explanation of each

Close Reading and Writing Routine

In each unit, you will read texts that share a common theme, despite their different genres, time periods, and authors. Each reading encourages a closer look through questions and a short writing assignment.

1 Introduction

An Introduction to each text provides historical context for your reading as well as information about the author. You will also learn about the genre of the text and the year in which it was written.

2 Notes

Many times, while working through the activities after each text, you will be asked to **annotate** or **make annotations** about what you are reading. This means that you should highlight or underline words in the text and use the "Notes" column to make comments or jot down any questions you have. You may also want to note any unfamiliar vocabulary words here.

You will also see sample student annotations to go along with the Skill lesson for that text.

First Read

During your first reading of each selection, you should just try to get a general idea of the content and message of the reading. Don't worry if there are parts you don't understand or words that are unfamiliar to you. You'll have an opportunity later to dive deeper into the text.

Think Questions

These questions will ask you to start thinking critically about the text, asking specific questions about its purpose, and making connections to your prior knowledge and reading experiences. To answer these questions, you should go back to the text and draw upon specific evidence to support your responses. You will also begin to explore some of the more challenging vocabulary words in the selection.

Skills

Each Skill includes two parts: Checklist and Your Turn. In the Checklist, you will learn the process for analyzing the text. The model student annotations in the text provide examples of how you might make your own notes following the instructions in the Checklist. In the Your Turn, you will use those same instructions to practice the skill.

 First Read

Read "The Tell-Tale Heart." After you read, complete the Think Questions below.

THINK QUESTIONS

1. Write two or three sentences explaining how the narrator feels about the old man and why he decides to murder him.

2. Does the narrator seem trustworthy as he gives his account of the events in the story? Cite evidence from the text to explain your opinions.

3. What sound does the narrator hear at the end of the story that causes him to confess to the murder? Provide evidence to support your inference.

4. Find the word **sufficient** in paragraph 3 of "The Tell-Tale Heart." Use context clues in the surrounding sentences, as well as the sentence in which the word appears, to determine the word's meaning. Write your definition here and identify clues that helped you figure out its meaning.

5. Use context clues to determine the meaning of **sagacity** as it is used in paragraph 4 of "The Tell-Tale Heart." Write your definition here and identify clues that helped you figure out its meaning. Then check the meaning in a dictionary.

The Tell-Tale Heart

LANGUAGE, STYLE, AND AUDIENCE

Skill:
Language, Style, and Audience

Use the Checklist to analyze Language, Style, and Audience in "The Tell-Tale Heart." Refer to the sample student annotations about Language, Style, and Audience in the text.

CHECKLIST FOR LANGUAGE, STYLE, AND AUDIENCE

In order to determine an author's style, do the following:

✓ identify and define any unfamiliar words or phrases

✓ use context, including the meanings of surrounding words and phrases

✓ note possible reactions to the author's word choice

✓ examine your reaction to the author's word choice

✓ identify any analogies, or comparisons in which one part of the comparison helps explain the other

To analyze the impact of specific word choice on meaning and tone, ask the following questions:

✓ How did your understanding of the language change during your analysis?

✓ How do the writer's word choices impact or create meaning in the text?

✓ How do the writer's word choices impact or create a specific tone in the text?

✓ How could various audiences interpret this language? What different possible emotional responses can you list?

✓ What analogies do you see? Where might an analogy have clarified meaning or created a specific tone?

YOUR TURN

1. What effect do the punctuation choices in paragraphs 9 and 10 have on the tone?
   - ○ A. The dashes and exclamation marks reveal that the narrator is losing control.
   - ○ B. The italics make it clear that the narrator's words aren't to be trusted.
   - ○ C. The semicolons introduce a formal tone into an informal speech.
   - ○ D. The frequent questions reveal the narrator's attempt to engage the reader.

2. Which phrase from the passage most clearly suggests the narrator's disturbed mental state at the end of the story?
   - ○ A. "but I talked more fluently"
   - ○ B. "Why would they not be gone?"
   - ○ C. "It grew louder—louder—louder!"
   - ○ D. "And still the men chatted pleasantly"

6

Close Read & Skills Focus

After you have completed the First Read, you will be asked to go back and read the text more closely and critically. Before you begin your Close Read, you should read through the Skills Focus to get an idea of the concepts you will want to focus on during your second reading. You should work through the Skills Focus by making annotations, highlighting important concepts, and writing notes or questions in the "Notes" column. Depending on instructions from your teacher, you may need to respond online or use a separate piece of paper to start expanding on your thoughts and ideas.

Write

Your study of each selection will end with a writing assignment. For this assignment, you should use your notes, annotations, personal ideas, and answers to both the Think and Skills Focus Questions. Be sure to read the prompt carefully and address each part of it in your writing.

English Language Learner

The English Language Learner texts focus on improving language proficiency. You will practice learning strategies and skills in individual and group activities to become better readers, writers, and speakers.

Reading & Writing
Companion

Extended Writing Project and Grammar

This is your opportunity to use genre characteristics and craft to compose meaningful, longer written works exploring the theme of each unit. You will draw information from your readings, research, and own life experiences to complete the assignment.

1 Writing Project

After you have read all of the unit text selections, you will move on to a writing project. Each project will guide you through the process of writing your essay. Student models will provide guidance and help you organize your thoughts. One unit ends with an **Extended Oral Project** which will give you an opportunity to develop your oral language and communication skills.

2 Writing Process Steps

There are four steps in the writing process: Plan, Draft, Revise, and Edit and Publish. During each step, you will form and shape your writing project, and each lesson's peer review will give you the chance to receive feedback from your peers and teacher.

3 Writing Skills

Each Skill lesson focuses on a specific strategy or technique that you will use during your writing project. Each lesson presents a process for applying the skill to your own work and gives you the opportunity to practice it to improve your writing.

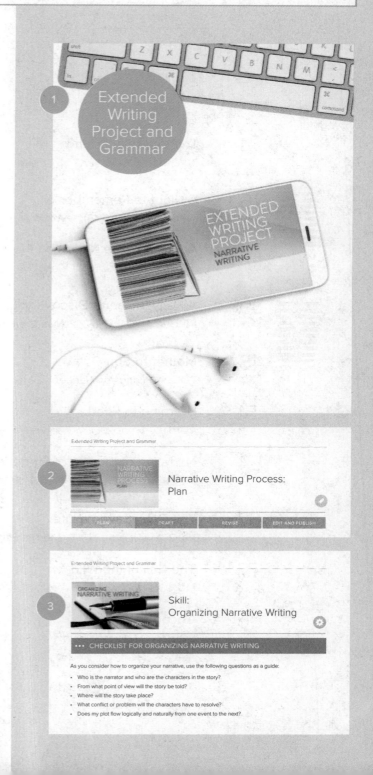

No Risk, No Reward

Why do we take chances?

Genre Focus: INFORMATIONAL

Texts

Paired Readings

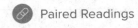

Reading & Writing Companion

Extended Writing Project and Grammar

Reading & Writing
Companion

Unit 3: No Risk, No Reward
Why do we take chances?

FREDERICK DOUGLASS

Born into slavery in Talbot County, Maryland, Frederick Douglass (ca. 1818–1895) was twenty years old when he escaped to freedom and became an active abolitionist. He taught himself to read despite laws prohibiting enslaved people from doing so, and only seven years after attaining his freedom, published the first of his three memoirs, *Narrative of the Life of Frederick Douglass, An American Slave* (1845). An account of his journey from slavery to freedom, it played a key role in fueling the abolitionist movement prior to the Civil War.

ANYA GRONER

A resident of New Orleans, Louisiana, Anya Groner has written essays, stories, and poems covering a wide range of subjects, from her childhood growing up in Virginia to the politics of drinking water. In "The Vanishing Island" (2017), Groner discusses the plight of the Native American inhabitants of the Isle de Jean Charles off the coast of Louisiana, as rising water levels threaten their ancestral homeland.

FRANCES ELLEN WATKINS HARPER

Writer, abolitionist, and civil rights activist Frances Ellen Watkins Harper (1825–1911) is credited with establishing the tradition of African American protest poetry. Born a free woman in Baltimore, Maryland, Harper traveled extensively throughout the eastern United States, often under hazardous circumstances, to voice her opposition to slavery and to advocate for the burgeoning feminist movement. As a result of her constant effort to raise awareness around these issues, she was elected vice president of the National Association of Colored Women in 1897.

LANGSTON HUGHES

Now regarded as a leading figure of the 1920's cultural and intellectual movement known as the Harlem Renaissance, Langston Hughes (1902–1967) initially faced widespread criticism from African American intellectuals for his unvarnished portrayals of African American life in his poetry. Despite the criticism he received, he maintained his commitment to writing for and about regular people throughout his life, earning him the moniker "poet of the people."

JACK LONDON

Turn-of-the-century American novelist and short-story writer Jack London (1876–1916) is best known for his novels *The Call of the Wild* (1903) and *White Fang* (1906) about wild wolf dogs in the Yukon Territory and the Northwest Territories of Canada during the Klondike Gold Rush of the 1890s. Writing between the Civil War and World War I, London's work reflected the nation's transformation into a modern, industrial society, and appealed to readers desiring a sense of adventure and vitality.

THOMAS PONCE

An animal rights activist and citizen lobbyist from Casselberry, Florida, Thomas Ponce (b. 2000) became a vegetarian at age four, attended his first protest at age five, and founded the animal rights organization Lobby For Animals at age twelve. He now works as a coordinator for Fin Free Florida, working to limit the sale, distribution, and trade of shark fins and shark fin products in the state of Florida. For his dedication to animal rights, he has received awards from major organizations like PETA and the Farm Animal Rights Movement.

RONALD REAGAN

Though he had an average, midwestern upbringing, Ronald Reagan (1911–2004) became the fortieth president of the United States and is the only Hollywood actor ever to become president. He is remembered for his conservative political beliefs and his policies toward the dissolution of Soviet communism. A major event of his presidency was the explosion of the Space Shuttle *Challenger* resulting in the deaths of its seven passengers. His address to the nation on January 28, 1986, lauded the bravery of the fallen crew.

MAHVASH SABET

Teacher, principal, and Bahá'í community leader Mahvash Sabet (b. 1953) was fired from her job and blocked from working in public education following the Islamic Revolution of 1979. She and the rest of the seven leaders that comprised an informal council working to support Iran's 300,000-member Bahá'í community were arrested in 2008. While serving her twenty-year prison sentence, she began writing poetry, and in 2013 published her first collection in English translation.

NINA GREGORY

Throughout her career, news editor and journalist Nina Gregory has covered topics ranging from the financial crisis to elections and has interviewed many influential figures including director Ava DuVernay and Facebook COO Sheryl Sandberg. One of her most intriguing stories profiles Richard Turere, a young boy living among the Maasai people near Nairobi National Park, a refuge for endangered lions in Kenya. As a thirteen-year-old, Turere came up with an inventive solution for protecting both the locals' livestock and the encroaching lions.

WALTER LORD

Walter Lord (1917–2002) had been obsessed with the story of the RMS *Titanic* since he came across a small book written by a survivor of the shipwreck in his aunt's home in 1927. Lord studied American and modern European history at Princeton University, but it wasn't until an editor friend suggested he turn his obsession with the Titanic into a book that he undertook the endeavor. With *A Night to Remember* (1955), Lord popularized the story and developed an innovative technique of telling history through the eyes of those who lived it.

The Vanishing Island

INFORMATIONAL TEXT
Anya Groner
2017

Introduction

Author Anya Groner offers an intimate perspective of the Biloxi-Chitimacha-Choctaw Native American tribe and the trials they face as their ancestral homeland disappears before their eyes. As creeping water threatens the tribe and much of the Louisiana coast, the tribe must take on the challenge of seeking a new and safe place to live. In a race against the clock, the tribe seeks ways to preserve community and protect their culture from eroding along with the land.

"We know we are going to lose it. We just don't know when."

The Lay of the Land

NOTES

Skill:
Media

1   At first glance, the Isle de Jean Charles, a skinny, two-mile long Louisiana island 75 miles south of New Orleans, looks like a tropical paradise. Beards of Spanish moss sway from the branches of oak trees. Orange and white wildflowers brighten both sides of the only street. Snow-white egrets, blue and green herons, and ebony anhingas stretch their necks, balancing on fallen trees. A flock of red-winged blackbirds takes flight, swooping before landing on the power lines. Even the houses have a bird-like quality. Teal, maroon, and gray, the buildings perch on stilts, fourteen feet off the ground. Wide porches and open front doors welcome visitors. A group has gathered for a fresh crawfish and crab boil. Everyone knows each other here: they grew up together, fishing and crabbing and catching game. Of the two dozen families that still live here, most are relatives and members of the Biloxi-Chitimacha-Choctaw Native American tribe. But the island is not what it used to be. In fact, the island is vanishing. By 2050, Isle de Jean Charles may be completely gone.

The boldface text sitting on its own line shows that this is a heading. The heading gives clues about the information in this section. The word land *indicates it will be about the geography of the island.*

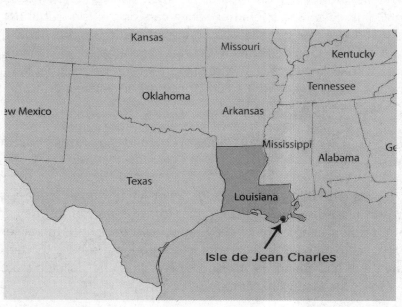

Isle de Jean Charles

Copyright © BookheadEd Learning, LLC

2 "Way back in the old days," lifetime resident Wenceslaus Billiot Sr. says in the film *Can't Stop the Waters,* "you had trees. There was no bay. All this water used to be marsh." Billiot Sr. is an 89-year-old boat builder and lifelong resident who has watched the landscape transform. "I built this house in the 1960s. I have another I built in '49. I built it all." Since 1955, the tribe has lost 98 percent of their land to encroaching waters. What was once an eleven-by-five mile island that contained forests and cattle farms is now just two miles long and a quarter of a mile wide. The land, composed of soft, silty dirt, has dissolved, much of it giving way to the waters of the Gulf of Mexico—and the population has shrunk along with the island.

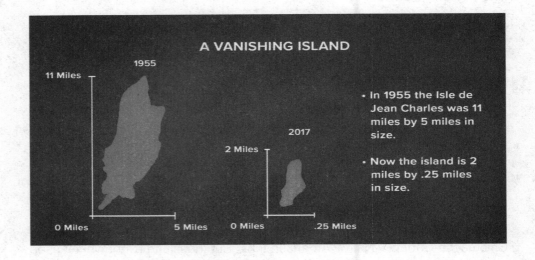

3 "Just in my lifetime, the amount of land loss is astonishing," says tribal secretary Chantel Comardelle. She spent her early years on the island, but her family left when she was four because life on the mainland is more stable than an uncertain future on Isle de Jean Charles. Nonetheless, like many tribal members who've moved away, the island remains her cultural home. She visits nearly every weekend, usually bringing her children with her. "Every time I go back, I see a little bit less."

4 "I grew up here," echoes Emray Naquin. "The land is going like you wouldn't believe."

5 When he was a child, the tribe's leader, Chief Albert Naquin, set traps in the woods with his father. Now, though, that forest is part of the bay, a place where fishermen search for crabs. Farms have vanished, too. There's no place for livestock. Even small vegetable gardens are hard to keep. Over time, the earth has absorbed salt and arsenic from the polluted waters that sweep across the land with increasing frequency.

6   "We were so self-sufficient as a tribe, that [in the past] we were unaware of the outside world," explains Damian Naquin. He's eighteen years old. He grew up in nearby Pointe-aux-Chenes. "When the Great Depression happened, the tribe didn't know it." He says that during the nation's greatest economic collapse, tribe members suffered no shortage of food. "It didn't affect us."

7   Self-sufficiency used to be a point of pride for islanders who found freedom in working for themselves. **Subsistence**, the ability to live off one's natural surroundings, is no longer possible because of land loss. The forests are gone, and without the marshes to sustain fish nurseries and provide habitats, the once abundant sea life has diminished.

8   "At one time, water was our life. Now it's almost our enemy because it is driving us out," says Comardelle. "It's a double-edged sword. Our life and our death."

9   Between August and October, the peak months of hurricane season, day-to-day erosion is worsened by storms. Since 1998, Terrebonne Parish, the region that encompasses the Isle de Jean Charles, has suffered a federally-declared disaster every two years. The big ones arrive with more strength and more frequency than in the past. The natural features that used to protect land—wetlands and barrier island—are gone. During hurricanes, waist-deep water rises over the only exit road, cutting off the island from rescue crews. Trees fall and wind rips walls and roofs from buildings. Before residents began elevating their homes atop stilts, biannual flood waters swept furniture and belongings into the bay. "Every time there's a flood, we lose everything," explains Damian. "We don't have any valuables. We know, if we get something, the next storm that comes through, it's going to ruin it. It's going to carry it away."

10   When storms subside, weary residents paddle through town checking up on one another and assessing the damage. After the waters recede, mold and mildew linger, which causes respiratory problems and makes residents ill. The cycle of devastation and rebuilding is exhausting. But it wasn't always like this.

11   "Now [folks] evacuate for hurricanes. Back then they didn't," recalls Comardelles's father, Deputy Chief Wenceslaus Billiot Jr. As a child in 1965, he spent Hurricane Betsy in his father's boat, in the canal in front of their house. "We would get hit by storms but it wouldn't be as bad because we had protection. When Camille hit we didn't have any damage at all. Now, a hurricane like Betsy hits? Shooo." His voice drops to a whisper and he shakes his head.

12   With such severe conditions, outsiders are often baffled to learn that many of the remaining residents of Isle de Jean Charles refuse to leave. The island, which some affectionately refer to as "the bathtub," isn't simply a place to

Please note that excerpts and passages in the StudySync® library and this workbook are intended as touchstones to generate interest in an author's work. The excerpts and passages do not substitute for the reading of entire texts, and StudySync® strongly recommends that students seek out and purchase the whole literary or informational work in order to experience it as the author intended. Links to online resellers are available in our digital library. In addition, complete works may be ordered through an authorized reseller by filling out and returning to StudySync® the order form enclosed in this workbook.

Reading & Writing Companion   3

NOTES

live—it is the center of tribal life and a cultural homeland. Eight generations have grown up on Isle de Jean Charles, surviving off the bounty of the water and land around them: hunting, fishing, trapping, and gardening. As the land **erodes**, the Biloxi-Chitimacha-Choctaw tribal culture erodes with it. "Once our island goes, the core of our tribe is lost," says Comardelle. "We've lost our whole culture—that is what is on the line."

13   Many elder tribe members don't want another way of life. They grew up here. Though the island has changed, giving up on their homeland is simply too hard. For them, staying put is a way of maintaining traditional life. Others lack the financial resources to live elsewhere. They have come to terms with cleaning up flood damage every two to three years.

14   Island life has changed dramatically over the past few decades. "The old chief, a great-great-great-grandpa of mine, he owned the [island] store," remembers Comardelle. "The store was also the dance hall, it was the church, it was the wedding hall, it was everything." When the population began shrinking, the store shut down. Today the closest grocery store is fifteen miles away. Other community spaces have disappeared as well. There are no longer event grounds on the island. Grand Bois Park, a public event space on the mainland once used for pow wows, has been destroyed by flooding, too. The tribe hasn't held a pow wow—a traditional Native American festival—since before Hurricane Katrina hit Louisiana in 2005. "We have no place," says Comardelle. "I used to dance in pow wow dress. My kids have never experienced that."

15   What remains are the Isle de Jean Charles firehouse and the local marina. Above the tin roof, an orange flag flaps in the wind. It is the flag of Houma Nation, the name of another local Native American tribe. On weekends, visitors come to the island to eat fresh crawfish, shrimp, and crabs; the rest of the week the marina is quiet, as though already abandoned.

16   For more than fifteen years, Chief Naquin has been trying to relocate his people. "The longer we wait," Naquin says in the documentary *Can't Stop the Water*, "the more hurricane seasons we have to go through. We hate to let the island go, but we have to. It's like losing a family member. We know we are going to lose it. We just don't know when."

17   As chief, Naquin believes he must have a good heart in order to know right from wrong and determine what's good for his people. "We're washing away, one day at a time," he says. It is painful for him to admit, but Naquin believes the tribe's future lies elsewhere.

18   In January of 2016, Chief Naquin received good news. Through a Housing and Urban Development grant, his tribe received $48 million, about half the

estimated cost of resettling the tribe. The money would help build a community center, medical facilities, and housing for tribe members. That includes the 600 or so people who left Isle de Jean Charles and scattered throughout Louisiana. The grant would also help fund an education program so visitors can learn about the island's history and the difficult process of relocation.

19 "I'm flying high as a kite," Naquin told the newspaper *Houma Today* after receiving the news. It's easy to understand why the grant would make him so happy. Though the island is vanishing, with this money the Biloxi-Chitimacha-Choctaw tribe just may have a future.

Eight Generations of History

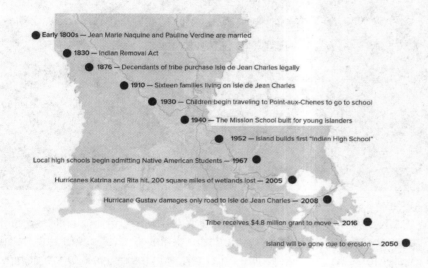

- Early 1800s — Jean Marie Naquine and Pauline Verdine are married
- 1830 — Indian Removal Act
- 1876 — Decendants of tribe purchase Isle de Jean Charles legally
- 1910 — Sixteen families living on Isle de Jean Charles
- 1930 — Children begin traveling to Point-aux-Chenes to go to school
- 1940 — The Mission School built for young islanders
- 1952 — Island builds first "Indian High School"
- Local high schools begin admitting Native American Students — 1967
- Hurricanes Katrina and Rita hit. 200 square miles of wetlands lost — 2005
- Hurricane Gustav damages only road to Isle de Jean Charles — 2008
- Tribe receives $4.8 million grant to move — 2016
- Island will be gone due to erosion — 2050

20 Jean Marie Naquin and Pauline Verdin married in the early 1800s. After their wedding, though, they needed to hide: Jean Marie was French and Pauline was Native American. At the time in Louisiana, interracial couples faced discrimination and even violence. Jean Marie's family disowned him because of the marriage. To escape persecution, Jean Marie and Pauline built their home on an "uninhabited" island. The landscape was rich with palmettos, alligators, crawfish, and sea birds.

21 Ironically, it was Jean Marie's disapproving father, Jean Charles, for whom the Isle de Jean Charles was likely named. He was the one who first showed his son the island, hidden in the coastal wetlands. Jean Charles had first come to the island while he was employed by the notorious privateer and outlaw, Jean Lafitte. At the time, Louisiana's wetlands were considered "uninhabitable" by the government. They weren't even mapped by Europeans. For a man like Jean Lafitte, a privateer who transported stolen goods and slaves to illegal markets, the maze of marshes provided a hiding place for his misdeeds.

Please note that excerpts and passages in the StudySync® library and this workbook are intended as touchstones to generate interest in an author's work. The excerpts and passages do not substitute for the reading of entire texts, and StudySync® strongly recommends that students seek out and purchase the whole literary or informational work in order to experience it as the author intended. Links to online resellers are available in our digital library. In addition, complete works may be ordered through an authorized reseller by filling out and returning to StudySync® the order form enclosed in this workbook.

Reading & Writing Companion   **5**

22   The coastal swamps provided safety for the newly married Jean Marie and Pauline. Not only was the island isolated, the land was also free. "Uninhabitable" land meant unwanted land, so Jean Marie and Pauline simply claimed it as their own. They built their home from mud, moss, and palmetto leaves, a kind of construction known as bousillage. Soon they started a family.

23   By the 1830s, Jean Marie and Pauline's children were having children of their own. Later, they married Native Americans from off the island and brought them to Isle de Jean Charles to live and start families as well. Once again, the remote location provided safety from a hostile society. In 1830, the United States Congress passed the Indian Removal Act, a federal law authorizing the forced removal of southern Native Americans from their ancestral land. The purpose of the law was to enable white settlers to move in. A few tribes, including the Mississippi Choctaws, signed treaties exchanging their homeland for payment and land rights west of the Mississippi. Other tribes resisted and the situation escalated. White men formed local and state militias, which forced southern and southeastern Native Americans to abandon their homes and march west to Oklahoma and Texas. The Native Americans were exposed to the elements. They lacked supplies. Thousands died and the march west became known as the Trail of Tears, in memory of the lives and culture lost.

24   Unlike so many other Native Americans, the growing Naquin family escaped the Trail of Tears because of their hidden island deep in the marshes. For the second time, the swamp saved their lives.

25 By 1876, Louisiana settlers were looking to expand their communities and build in new places. The state revoked the coastal marshes' official designation as "uninhabitable." It put the wetlands and their hidden islands up for sale. Four families, residents of Isle de Jean Charles and descendants of Jean Marie and Pauline, purchased the land they lived on, which gave them a legal claim to the island their families had been occupying for seven decades.

26 By 1910, sixteen families lived on Isle de Jean Charles. Residents were fluent in Cajun French and English. They lived a subsistence-based lifestyle. Families fished, trapped, and hunted for food. They added to their diets with gardens. They had domesticated livestock such as chickens and cows.

27 French, Native American, and African food cultures influenced their cuisine. For instance, Gumbo Fricassee, a popular dish, contains the following ingredients:

- Okra - a vegetable imported from West Africa during the slave trade
- Roux - a mixture of fat and flour often used as a base in French cooking
- Filé - a Choctaw spice made from ground sassafras leaves
- The Holy Trinity - a Catholic nickname for the celery, bell peppers, and onions, essential ingredients in any gumbo recipe
- Whatever seafood, chicken, or sausage is fresh and available

28 Religious practices on the island similarly combine French Catholic and Native American customs. To this day, many Biloxi-Chitimacha-Choctaw people attend both church and pow wows.

29 Masculinity was important in both games and government. On Christian or Native American holidays, men and boys often gathered to play pick, a game still played today. Damiann Naquin first played pick when he was six. Pick, he explains, is "a simple game. You have a circle in the mud. Everyone has a sharpened wooden stick, which you find from a tree and sharpen. . . . The point [is] to see who could keep their stick in the mud the longest [and] to knock another person's stick down."

30 The tribe's chief was always a man. As the tribal leader, he would **maintain** the grocery store, distribute mail, help **settle** disputes, represent the people of the island to outsiders, and gather residents for community service. Upon retirement, he chose his successor, a practice that continues to this day.

31 Despite the growing size of the community, for decades Isle de Jean Charles lacked a school. In the 1930s, children began traveling by small wooden boats called pirogues to the nearby town of Pointe-aux-Chenes, where a missionary school funded by donations and run by the Live Oak Baptist Church served both white and Native American children. At that time, though, Louisiana was committed to Jim Crow laws, which legalized racial segregation. The missionary school didn't last long. The superintendent visited, saw a racially mixed classroom, and shut the school down. The island children had nowhere to go.

32   In 1940, Baptists tried again to provide education for the younger islanders by building the Mission School. It was a one room building on the Isle de Jean Charles. The mission school filled a gap, but it only ran to eighth grade. Eventually, some frustrated families moved off the island. In 1952, Louisiana built its first "Indian High School" in Houma, Louisiana. It was a segregated school for Native American teenagers 25 miles from Isle de Jean Charles. It was not until 1967 that local public schools admitted Native American students.

Please note that excerpts and passages in the StudySync® library and this workbook are intended as touchstones to generate interest in an author's work. The excerpts and passages do not substitute for the reading of entire texts, and StudySync® strongly recommends that students seek out and purchase the whole literary or informational work in order to experience it as the author intended. Links to online resellers are available in our digital library. In addition, complete works may be ordered through an authorized reseller by filling out and returning to StudySync® the order form enclosed in this workbook.

Reading & Writing Companion   9

**Skill:
Media**

The author talks about the road being low and easily flooded and then includes a photograph of it. The photo really helps me see how close to the water the road is. No one could get to school or work when it floods.

33 Even today, there are no schools on the island. The closest schools are on the mainland. In 2008, Hurricane Gustav damaged the only road connecting the mainland to the island, turning it from a two-lane road into a one-lane road. After that, school buses stopped coming to Isle de Jean Charles. All but one family with school-age children have moved away. Though the road has been repaired, it still sits only inches above open water. High winds can cause flooding over the pavement. "If you live on the island and the road is flooded then you can't go to school or go to work," explains Sheila Billiot.

Stomping Out the Boot

34 If you open a United States atlas or search the Internet for "Louisiana map," you'll discover a state shaped roughly like a boot. Louisiana is bordered by the Mississippi River to the east, Arkansas to the north, and Texas to the west. The foot of the boot stretches south and east into the Gulf of Mexico.

**Skill:
Greek and
Latin Affixes
and Roots**

I see the word geological, and I think it has to do with a study of Earth. I know that it combines the Greek root geo, meaning "earth," and the Greek root logy, meaning "the study of."

35 A state's shape sounds unchangeable, but some Louisianans believe their map needs to be redrawn. "The boot is at best an inaccurate approximation," writes Brett Anderson, staff writer for the New Orleans newspaper *The Times-Picayune.* Anderson isn't disputing Louisiana's borders with surrounding states; his contention lies with the southernmost border, where the state's marshy edges are rapidly slipping into the gulf.

36 Because marshlands are largely impassable except by boat, it's difficult to understand the magnitude of Louisiana's land loss unless viewing it from a plane. The United States Geological Service (USGS) reports that between 1932 and 2000, roughly 1,900 square miles of Louisiana's land vanished into the Gulf of Mexico. That's an area about the size of Delaware. Today, an

estimated football field of land is lost every 45 minutes. That rate of land loss is higher than almost anywhere else on the planet. If no measures are put in place to prevent more erosion, another 1,750 square miles—a landmass larger than Rhode Island—will give way by 2064. "Our coast is going away faster than pretty much any other coast in the world," explains Pat Forbes. He's the Executive Director of the Louisiana State Office of Community and Development. Currently, Louisiana's greatest land loss occurs during storms. In 2005, the year Hurricanes Katrina and Rita hit, Louisiana lost more than 200 square miles of coastal wetlands in a single summer.

Louisiana Shoreline Change 1937-2000

37   In addition to hurricane damage and global sea level rise, other factors also contribute to land loss. The engineering of the Mississippi River, the land's natural propensity to sink and erode, and the dredging of canals throughout the wetlands have also contributed to the loss of land in Louisiana.

38   From its source in Minnesota, the Mississippi River winds its way through nine more states before spilling into the Gulf of Mexico: Wisconsin, Iowa, Illinois, Missouri, Kentucky, Tennessee, Arkansas, Mississippi, and Louisiana. The river, nicknamed the Big Muddy, picks up dirt and carries it downstream. Eventually, this dirt is deposited along the Louisiana Gulf Coast, a process that has replenished and maintained coastline marshes and islands that would otherwise erode into the sea. "Essentially," explains Forbes, "most of Southern Louisiana has been built up by sediment carried down the Mississippi over thousands of years." Without this sediment to constantly build back the land, Louisiana's coastline would naturally diminish.

39   In 1927, unusually heavy rains overwhelmed the Mississippi River, flooding an area the size of Ireland and causing the current to run backwards. Levees broke. Floodwaters swept away farms and towns. In some places the swollen river stretched more than 60 miles wide. More than 700,000 people lost their homes. The damage cost about $1 billion at the time to fix.

40 To prevent such a disaster from happening again, the US government constructed the world's largest river containment system around the Big Muddy. The Army Corps of Engineers built dirt barriers called levees on either side of the river to prevent the floodwaters from spilling over the banks. They also dug man-made canals, called floodways. That way, when the river swelled, the water could be released along predictable routes. Rather than carving a new riverbed every spring, as the Mississippi had done annually since the last Ice Age, the massive waterway was given a fixed path which ended in the Gulf of Mexico.

41 The levees and floodways prevented the Mississippi from overflowing its banks, but they also stopped the river from carrying out many of the natural processes that surrounding states relied on. The levee system cut the Louisiana coast off from the sediment that nourished and created the land. The dirt that gave the Big Muddy its nickname no longer reached Louisiana's marshes.

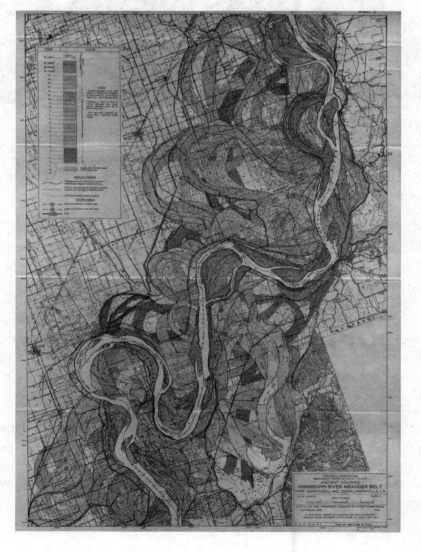

42 The problems caused by river engineering are worsened by subsidence, or the natural propensity for wetlands to sink and erode. Louisiana contains 40% of the nation's wetlands. These marshes make up more than a third of the state. They provide habitats for shrimp, fish, crawfish, and crabs. These animals are crucial to Louisiana's fisheries. Built from soft mud, these wetlands are constantly sinking and eroding, a natural process called subsidence. When the river dumps sediment into the marshes, the wetlands rebuild and the lost land replenishes. Without river sediment to continually build them back up, Louisiana's wetlands shrink, then vanish, a process that's been charted repeatedly along the coast.

43 In addition to subsidence, a system of canals crisscrosses the state's wetlands, further damaging the fragile ecosystem. In the swamp, these waterways function as roads, providing boats easy access to oil, gas, and fisheries; over time, however, they've created pathways for saltwater from the Gulf of Mexico to leach into the freshwater wetlands. Salt is poisonous to wetland plants such as Cypress and Tupelo Gum trees. As the flora dies off, the wetlands give way to open water.

44 The disappearance of the wetlands has had another unintended consequence. Marshes and swamps are like sponges; they can expand and soak up water, protecting the mainland and inland islands from storm surges and flooding— but without wetlands to provide natural barriers, hurricane damage can be even more **catastrophic.**

45 For Louisianans, restoring the coast is a race against time. The goal is not only to protect the land, but also to care for the humans, plants, and animals that live there. The US economy is deeply linked to Louisiana's wellbeing. The state's commercial fishing industry produces a quarter of US seafood, and nearly half of the nation's grain supply passes through the port of New Orleans. Since 2007, the state has built 250 miles of levees and constructed 45 miles of barrier islands and berms. But this massive effort has not been able to keep up with the rate of land loss.

Stay or Go?

46 The first opportunity for the Biloxi-Chitimacha-Choctaw tribe to relocate came in 2002. The Army Corps of Engineers redrew the path of the Morganza-to-the-Gulf Levee. This 98-mile earthen wall was designed to protect people and property from hurricanes and storm surges. Originally, Isle de Jean Charles was included in this plan. The levee would keep water off the island and the land would regenerate. However, in 2002, the Army Corps of Engineers decided to bypass Isle de Jean Charles. For islanders, the news was devastating.

Please note that excerpts and passages in the StudySync® library and this workbook are intended as touchstones to generate interest in an author's work. The excerpts and passages do not substitute for the reading of entire texts, and StudySync® strongly recommends that students seek out and purchase the whole literary or informational work in order to experience it as the author intended. Links to online resellers are available in our digital library. In addition, complete works may be ordered through an authorized reseller by filling out and returning to StudySync® the order form enclosed in this workbook.

Reading & Writing Companion   **13**

Skill:
Greek and
Latin Affixes
and Roots

I'm not sure what the word relocate means. I can tell it is a verb because the word to comes before it. I think it may have a Greek or Latin root, but I need to look it up to be sure.

Skill:
Greek and
Latin Affixes
and Roots

Relocation looks like relocate, so the words probably have a similar meaning. I know the suffix -ion forms nouns. Based on these clues, I think the word relocation might mean "the act of moving to a new place."

47 The Army Corps of Engineers offered to relocate the community. But it would only happen if the residents voted unanimously in favor of resettling. "The plan was dead in the water," Comardelle recalls. "At the time, we'd had a lot of land loss, but we hadn't had major structural issues [with buildings and infrastructure]." The majority of residents were in favor of the relocation. However, some residents, particularly tribal elders, were reluctant to leave. "It's home for them, you know," Dominick explains. "They were born, raised, grew up, lived their whole entire lives there. Even though their home is being stripped away, they still don't want to leave because of the sentimental value." Others worried the relocation was part of a dishonest effort to take over their island. In the end, the tribe couldn't get unanimous support. The relocation was voted down by the people.

48 Several years after the vote, storm damage caused tribe members to reconsider their stance. In 2005, Hurricanes Katrina and Rita flooded the island, badly damaging the land. Three years later, when Hurricane Gustav hit Isle de Jean Charles directly, houses lost roofs and walls, gas lines broke, and the utility company refused to replace the lines. Many residents left, and those who stayed behind reconsidered their options.

49 In 2009, the tribal council restarted the relocation process. This time, plans progressed much further. Most residents were ready to leave. The tribal

council found land to purchase. This time the relocation was halted by their future neighbors. "We were going forward and some issues came up with the [adjacent] neighborhood," remembers Comardelle. "That community rose up and said they didn't want [us] in their backyard." With no place to move, tribe members wondered if their culture was fated to vanish along with the island.

50   Good news came in early 2016. That's when the Biloxi-Chitimacha-Choctaw tribe learned they would receive the $48 million relocation grant from the federal office of Housing and Urban Development. Beginning with the marriage of Jean Marie Naquin and Pauline Verdin, eight generations of tribal members made their home on the Isle de Jean Charles. The relocation grant meant the tribe could have a future, but it would have to be elsewhere. Though he was thrilled to receive the grant, in an article in *National Geographic* Chief Naquin compared "losing the island" with "losing a family member."

51   Federal grants have supported resettlement projects for storm victims for decades. They've enabled, for example, families who lost houses in Hurricane Katrina and Hurricane Sandy to live elsewhere. The Isle de Jean Charles relocation, however, is an entirely new endeavor. "Resettling a community is entirely different from relocating individuals," explains Pat Forbes. "In the past, when an area's been declared unsafe to live, the state or federal government has offered buyouts to affected landowners. In other words, they pay residents to leave. The problem with buyouts is that communities don't stay together."

52   In contrast, the primary goal of the Isle de Jean Charles relocation is to preserve the community and culture of the Biloxi-Chitimacha-Choctaw tribe. Rather than splitting up tribe members, the grant aims to bring people together. The grant proposal explains, "The tribe has physically and culturally been torn apart with the scattering of members. . . . A new settlement offers an opportunity for the tribe to rebuild their homes and secure their culture on safe ground." With this funding, island residents and tribal members who left their homeland due to land loss and flooding can also rejoin their community in a new location.

53   "The people of the Isle de Jean Charles Band of Biloxi-Chitimacha-Choctaw tribe are situated on the front line of Louisiana's coastal land loss disaster and their ancestral home is sinking into the marsh," explains Forbes. "This $48 million grant will allow the state to help them resettle their entire community to a safer place with minimum of disruption to livelihoods and lifestyles.

Together we'll be creating a model for resettlement of endangered coastal communities throughout the United States."

54   To accomplish this lofty goal, tribal members have been dreaming big. "We could have our own community center," says secretary Comardelle. "We could have room to grow. We could have our own crops, our own industry if we wanted. We want to be our own place again."

55   Community members are working hard to make the relocation happen. "It's about family," says Dominick Naquin. "No matter how many times we've been shot down, we came back stronger and kept fighting." Perhaps everything that the Isle de Jean Charles' residents and their ancestors have overcome has set them up for this moment. With ancestors who escaped the Trail of Tears and families who've survived numerous hurricanes, they're well equipped to triumph despite unfavorable odds.

A Vision of Community

56   "I want you to feel like you have just walked onto the original island, with the way the trees look, the way the vegetation looks," says Chantel Comardelle. She's leaning back in a brown armchair in her two-bedroom house in Houma, Louisiana, 45 minutes from the Isle de Jean Charles. To her right sits her daughter's three-story plastic dollhouse; to her left, giant containers filled with quilts and photo albums. Heirlooms inherited when her mother-in-law passed away. One room over, one of her young sons is crying. Comardelle's mother, Sheila Billiot, is talking to him softly, comforting him. The emphasis on family, a value nearly every member of her tribe seems to cherish, is abundant in this house.

57   Comardelle's eyes are closed as she talks. Physically, she's here, in her living room. Spiritually, she's in the future, imagining what her tribe's relocation will look like. What will it mean for her family and for the future of her people? Her voice is confident as if she's describing a place that already exists.

58   "When you pull up, when you approach the community, the center grounds are also pow wow grounds." In the front of the facility, she imagines a museum. It's a wooden building with a front porch. When visitors enter, they feel like they're walking into someone's house. "I want guests to walk through the history of the island with the original settlers. The ceiling, I want it to be the road to show how it progressed. With no road, just water and canoes, and then you have the road, and then you start to see the road on the floor. I want to have a big map on the wall and show the island. I want it to be digitized to show you how the island's progressed in digital pictures as far as land loss, how it's shrunk."

59 Comardelle's belief in the museum is so great that she's begun taking online graduate courses in museum studies, using her class assignments to start planning exhibits and features. "Even the sounds will be like you're on the island," she says. "I want French music playing in some sections. I want people talking in other sections. I want animal sounds in other sections. I want you to be fully immersed." Comardelle's vision is so detailed and her belief so firm that it's hard to imagine the future panning out any other way.

60 Besides the museum, Comardelle imagines the new site hosting other public facilities. There will be a store, a clinic, and a restaurant. "We hope to have a kitchen. The food's traditional Cajun food. Gumbo. Gumbo fricassee. We're going to have a healthcare facility. We want to have a 24-hour nurse, and we'll also service the outside, so it'll be like a both-ways kind of thing. We also want to have a childcare facility. An elderly senior center. Our kitchen will cook and serve food for the outside, but daily they'll make a plate lunch for our residents who are elderly."

61 Comardelle's idealism is intentional. In 2010, the tribe began working with a non-profit called the Lowlander Center, a community-run organization aimed at helping lowland residents build a future while adapting to an ever-changing coastline. After Hurricane Gustav, volunteers at the Lowlander Center heard about the tribe's resettlement plan. They encouraged the council of elders to come up with their best-case scenario. "All the bells and whistles," recalls Comardelle. "Everything you want. Everything you desire."

62 Beyond the pow wow grounds, the museum, and the restaurant, Comardelle envisions a less public part of the community where residents live. Designed to accommodate up to 400 members, the houses will be arranged, as they were on the the island, so that extended families share backyards. Aunts and uncles and grandparents will be able watch each other's children. They'll call across to each other from porch to porch. "I want to build that family unit back," says Comardelle.

63 Comardelle isn't the only one to prioritize shared responsibility and familial interactions. At eighteen, Damian and Dominick Naquin are the youngest members of the resettlement committee. They see blood relationships as the glue that holds their community together.

64 "As a future, I would love to see us stay as a family," explains Damian. "Some elders don't want to give up what they remember, what they hold onto, but their grandchildren, they would love to see another future for them. They want to save the family values and the culture so that the younger generation can experience what they experienced."

65 "If we're successful with the relocation," adds Dominick, "then the elders will know the younger generation will experience what they experienced."

66 As for their own future, the twin brothers hope to return to their tribe equipped with skills to help their community thrive. Both are currently freshmen at Louisiana State University in Baton Rouge. "I'm trying to become a pediatrician, a child doctor," says Damian. "If I achieve that goal, I know I'm able to bring a very valuable resource back. I see my role in the future of the tribe, to support wherever the tribe goes."

67 Dominick, who's majoring in computer science, echoes his brother's wish to contribute to the well-being of his people. His ideal day in the new community includes multigenerational activities. "I'll wake up. I'll do my job, whatever that may be," he says. "Hopefully, when the time comes, I would have the privilege to sit down with a whole bunch of children and be able to sit down in a circle drum and teach them how to drum and sing. To pass down our culture, that would bring me great joy."

68 Damian and Dominick's plans are exactly what the tribe needs for the resettlement to work. Maintaining a cultural identity is the primary goal of the resettlement, but the only way that can happen is through interaction across age groups. Already, the culture is being lost. Comardelle's grandmother was a medicinal herbalist, who used teas and plants to cure others. Those skills weren't passed down and the tradition was lost.

69 Until the relocation is complete, Comardelle does her best to transfer culture by taking her children to Isle de Jean Charles, explaining, "If you can keep the younger generation connected with the oldest generation, you can keep that transition. I notice it with my kids, when we go visit my grandma. They're learning French in school and they're tickled to go over there and talk French with my grandma."

70 Perhaps, years from now, Comardelle's children will recall these trips to Isle de Jean Charles, an island homeland that no longer exists. Sitting on a back porch, they'll tell their children about how they caught crabs in the bayou. How they listened to their grandparents speak in Cajun French about weddings in general stores and waiting out hurricanes in their daddy's boats. Around them the egrets will take flight as Spanish moss sways in the breeze. Relatives might wave from nearby porches. After all, history isn't just what happened a long time ago. The creation of a new homeland, the tribe's relocation, and the council's efforts to maintain culture are all history in action. If the relocation works, Comardelle, the Naquins, and the other members of

Copyright © BookheadEd Learning, LLC

the Biloxi-Chitimacha-Choctaw tribe will achieve something amazing. Their people and their culture will have a safe home in coastal Louisiana for centuries to come.

NOTES

Anya Groner's essays and stories can be read in journals including *The New York Times, Ecotone, The Oxford American*, and *The Atlantic*. A resident of New Orleans, Groner teaches creative writing at the New Orleans Center for Creative Arts and through the New Orleans Writers Workshop.

First Read

Read "The Vanishing Island." After you read, complete the Think Questions below.

 THINK QUESTIONS

1. Why did people move to the Isle de Jean Charles? Provide two specific examples from the text to support your response.

2. Why is the Biloxi-Chitimacha-Choctaw tribe no longer able to subsist? Provide specific evidence from the text to support your response.

3. How does containment of the Mississippi River affect the Louisiana coastline? Provide specific evidence from the text to support your response.

4. Find the word **erodes** in paragraph 12 of "The Vanishing Island." Use context clues in the surrounding sentences, as well as the sentence in which the word appears, to determine the word's meaning. Write your definition here and identify clues that helped you figure out its meaning.

5. Read the following dictionary entry:

   settle
   set•tle \sedl\ *verb*

   a. to decide something
   b. to put things in order
   c. to move to a place to live
   d. to pay money that is owed
   e. to end an argument
   f. to get into a more comfortable position

   Which definition most closely matches the meaning of **settle** as it is used in paragraph 30? Write the correct definition of *settle* here and explain how you figured out the correct meaning.

Skill: Greek and Latin Affixes and Roots

Use the Checklist to analyze Greek and Latin Affixes and Roots in "The Vanishing Island." Refer to the sample student annotations about Greek and Latin Affixes and Roots in the text.

• • •   CHECKLIST FOR GREEK AND LATIN AFFIXES AND ROOTS

In order to identify Greek and Latin affixes and roots, note the following:

- ✓ the root
- ✓ the prefix and/or suffix

To use common, grade-appropriate Greek or Latin affixes and roots as clues to the meaning of a word, use the following questions as a guide:

- ✓ Can I identify the root of this word? Should I look in a dictionary or other resource?
- ✓ What is the meaning of the root?
- ✓ Can I identify the prefix and/or suffix of this word? Should I look in a dictionary or other resource?
- ✓ What is the meaning of the prefix and/or suffix?
- ✓ Does this affix change the word's part of speech?
- ✓ How do the word parts work together to define the word's meaning and part of speech?

Please note that excerpts and passages in the StudySync® library and this workbook are intended as touchstones to generate interest in an author's work. The excerpts and passages do not substitute for the reading of entire texts, and StudySync® strongly recommends that students seek out and purchase the whole literary or informational work in order to experience it as the author intended. Links to online resellers are available in our digital library. In addition, complete works may be ordered through an authorized reseller by filling out and returning to StudySync® the order form enclosed in this workbook.

Reading & Writing Companion   21

Skill: Greek and Latin Affixes and Roots

Reread paragraphs 15 and 21 of "The Vanishing Island." Then, using the Checklist on the previous page, answer the multiple-choice questions below.

↻ YOUR TURN

marina mar•in•a \mə ˈrē-nə\
Origin: from the Latin root *mar* meaning "sea"

local loc•al \lō-kəl\
Origin: from the Latin root *loc* meaning "place"

quiet qui•et \kwī-ət\
Origin: from the Latin root *qui* meaning "rest"

transport trans•port \tran(t)s-pôrt\
Origin: from the Latin root *trans* meaning "across" and *port* meaning "carry"

misdeed mis•deed \mis-dēd\
Origin: from the Greek root *mis* meaning "bad"

1. Based on its root, what is the most likely meaning of *marina* as it's used in the passage?

   ○ A. an island
   ○ B. to go swimming
   ○ C. a group of sailors
   ○ D. a dock in the water

2. Based on its root, what is the most likely meaning of *local* as it's used in the passage?

   ○ A. below
   ○ B. nearby
   ○ C. healthy
   ○ D. well-known

3. Based on its root, what is the most likely meaning of *quiet* as it's used in the passage?

   ○ A. calm
   ○ B. noisy
   ○ C. alive
   ○ D. asleep

4. Based on the Greek or Latin root, which of the words listed above best completes the following sentence?
   The men were on trial for several _____, including carrying money out of the country.

   ○ A. locals
   ○ B. marinas
   ○ C. misdeeds
   ○ D. transports

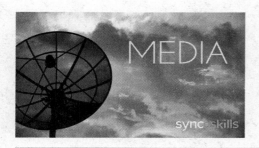

Skill:
Media

Use the Checklist to analyze Media in "The Vanishing Island." Refer to the sample student annotations about Media in the text.

••• CHECKLIST FOR MEDIA

In order to identify the advantages and disadvantages of using different media, note the following:

- ✓ the features of each medium, such as print or digital text, video, and multimedia

- ✓ how different media present a particular topic, idea, or historical event—such as World War II or the first moon landing—and can include diaries, eyewitness accounts, films, books, news and feature articles, photographs, and so on

- ✓ which details are stressed in each type of media presentation

- ✓ how readers and historians compare and contrast accounts in different media as they analyze and interpret events

- ✓ the reliability of each medium

- ✓ when presentations contradict each other

To evaluate the advantages and disadvantages of using different media to present a particular topic or idea, ask the following questions:

- ✓ What are the advantages and disadvantages of using different media to present a particular topic or idea?

- ✓ Which account of the event or topic is better supported by objective facts?

- ✓ Is an eyewitness account of an event more valuable than a film or book about the same subject? Why or why not?

Skill: Media

Reread paragraphs 20–22 of "The Vanishing Island." Then, using the Checklist on the previous page, answer the multiple-choice questions below.

⟳ YOUR TURN

1. Based on a text feature of the print medium in this excerpt, the reader can identify that the section is about—

   ○ A. the tribe's experiences on the island.
   ○ B. Native American traditions.
   ○ C. possible places for relocation.
   ○ D. environmental factors that affect the island.

2. The photograph in this excerpt provides information about—

   ○ A. Jean Lafitte.
   ○ B. how the island has changed.
   ○ C. how people on the island lived.
   ○ D. why the land was "uninhabitable."

3. The main advantage to including both types of media is that—

   ○ A. the photograph gives readers information that printed text cannot possibly give.
   ○ B. the two types of media work together to provide a clear idea and explanation for the reader's benefit.
   ○ C. it shows that the author did extensive research on the subject and is a reliable source of information.
   ○ D. the photograph helps break up the printed words on the page and makes it appear more readable.

Close Read

Reread "The Vanishing Island." As you reread, complete the Skills Focus questions below. Then use your answers and annotations from the questions to help you complete the Write activity.

◎ SKILLS FOCUS

1. The Latin root *duc* means "to lead." Identify a word with this root, and explain how the meaning of the root helps you understand the meaning of the word in context.

2. Identify a detail in the text that is clarified by a visual media item. Explain how the visual item deepens your understanding of the author's ideas.

3. For visual media items, what are some possible advantages and disadvantages of including them with the text? Be specific in your response and cite at least two examples for each situation.

4. Identify specific textual evidence that shows how relocation is a good way for the tribe to preserve their unique heritage. Explain your response.

5. Identify an example from some type of medium in "The Vanishing Island" of a risk members of the tribe took and explain why they took that chance.

✏ WRITE

INFORMATIVE: Based on the information in the article, what makes people care so deeply about this "vanishing island" that nothing can induce them to leave? Why do people still continue to inhabit it and work so hard for its cultural survival? Use evidence from the text, including different media, to support your understanding of the reading.

Please note that excerpts and passages in the StudySync® library and this workbook are intended as touchstones to generate interest in an author's work. The excerpts and passages do not substitute for the reading of entire texts, and StudySync® strongly recommends that students seek out and purchase the whole literary or informational work in order to experience it as the author intended. Links to online resellers are available in our digital library. In addition, complete works may be ordered through an authorized reseller by filling out and returning to StudySync® the order form enclosed in this workbook.

Reading & Writing Companion

25

A Night to Remember

INFORMATIONAL TEXT
Walter Lord
1955

Introduction

Walter Lord (1917–2002) interviewed scores of *Titanic* survivors to create a powerful account of the ship's sinking in the calm, frigid North Atlantic on April 14, 1912. In this passage, we hear a variety of reactions at the beginning of the disaster, from the first sighting of an iceberg by the ship's lookout to the mysterious jolt heard and felt by crew members and passengers alike, each

"It was almost 11:40 P.M. on Sunday, the 14th of April, 1912."

NOTES

from Chapter: "Another Belfast Trip"

1   High in the crow's-nest[1] of the New White Star Liner *Titanic,* Lookout Frederick Fleet peered into a dazzling night. It was calm, clear and bitterly cold. There was no moon, but the cloudless sky blazed with stars. The Atlantic was like polished plate glass; people later said they had never seen it so smooth.

2   This was the fifth night of the *Titanic's* maiden voyage to New York, and it was already clear that she was not only the largest but also the most **glamorous** ship in the world. Even the passengers' dogs were glamorous. John Jacob Astor had along his Airedale Kitty. Henry Sleeper Harper, of the publishing family, had his prize Pekingese Sun Yat-sen. Robert W. Daniel, the Philadelphia banker, was bringing back a champion French bulldog just purchased in Britain. Clarence Moore of Washington also had been dog-shopping, but the 50 pairs of English foxhounds he bought for the Loudoun Hunt weren't making the trip.

3   That was all another world to Frederick Fleet. He was one of six lookouts carried by the *Titanic,* and the lookouts didn't worry about passenger problems. They were the "eyes of the ship," and on this particular night Fleet had been warned to watch especially for icebergs.

4   So far, so good. On duty at 10 o'clock . . . a few words about the ice problem with Lookout Reginald Lee, who shared the same watch . . . a few more words about the cold . . . but mostly just silence, as the two men stared into the darkness.

5   Now the watch was almost over, and still there was nothing unusual. Just the night, the stars, the biting cold, the wind that whistled through the rigging as the *Titanic* raced across the calm, black sea at 22 1/2 knots[2]. It was almost 11:40 P.M. on Sunday, the 14th of April, 1912.

6   Suddenly Fleet saw something directly ahead, even darker than the darkness. At first it was small (about the size, he thought, of two tables put together), but every second it grew larger and closer. Quickly Fleet banged the crow's-nest

---

1. **crow's-nest** a platform on a ship's mast or in a high place used for lookout
2. **knot** a nautical mile

bell three times, the warning of danger ahead. At the same time he lifted the phone and rang the bridge.

7   "What did you see?" asked a calm voice at the other end.

8   "Iceberg right ahead," replied Fleet.

9   "Thank you," acknowledged the voice with curiously **detached** courtesy. Nothing more was said.

10   For the next 37 seconds, Fleet and Lee stood quietly side by side, watching the ice **draw** nearer. Now they were almost on top of it, and still the ship didn't turn. The berg towered wet and glistening far above the forecastle deck, and both men braced themselves for a crash. Then, miraculously, the bow began to swing to port. At the last second the stem shot into the clear, and the ice glided swiftly by along the starboard side. It looked to Fleet like a very close shave.

11   At this moment Quartermaster George Thomas Rowe was standing watch on the after bridge. For him too, it had been an uneventful night—just the sea, the stars, the biting cold. As he paced the deck, he noticed what he and his mates called "Whiskers 'round the Light"—tiny splinters of ice in the air, fine as dust, that gave off **myriads** of bright colors whenever caught in the glow of the deck lights.

12   Then suddenly he felt a curious motion break the steady rhythm of the engines. It was a little like coming alongside a dock wall rather heavily. He glanced forward—and stared again. A windjammer,[3] sails set, seemed to be passing along the starboard side. Then he realized it was an iceberg, towering perhaps 100 feet above the water. The next instant it was gone, drifting astern into the dark.

13   Meanwhile, down below in the First Class dining saloon on D Deck, four other members of the *Titanic's* crew were sitting around one of the tables. The last diner had long since departed, and now the big white Jacobean[4] room was empty except for this single group. They were dining-saloon stewards, indulging in the time-honored pastime of all stewards off duty—they were gossiping about their passengers.

14   Then, as they sat there talking, a faint grinding jar seemed to come from somewhere deep inside the ship. It was not much, but enough to break the conversation and rattle the silver that was set for breakfast next morning.

15   Steward James Johnson felt he knew just what it was. He recognized the kind of shudder a ship gives when she drops a propeller blade, and he knew this sort of mishap meant a trip back to the Harland & Wolff Shipyard at Belfast—with plenty of free time to enjoy the hospitality of the port.

---

3. **windjammer** a type of large sailing ship for passengers or cargo
4. **Jacobean** design or literature from Britain during the reign of King James IV (1567–1625)

16 Somebody near him agreed and sang out cheerfully, "Another Belfast trip!"

17 In the galley just to the stern, Chief Night Baker Walter Belford was making rolls for the following day. (The honor of baking fancy pastry was reserved for the day shift.) When the jolt came, it **impressed** Belford more strongly than Steward Johnson—perhaps because a pan of new rolls clattered off the top of the oven and scattered about the floor.

18 The passengers in their cabins felt the jar too, and tried to connect it with something familiar. Marguerite Frolicher, a young Swiss girl accompanying her father on a business trip, woke up with a start. Half-asleep, she could think only of the little white lake ferries at Zurich making a sloppy landing. Softly she said to herself, "Isn't it funny . . . we're landing!"

19 Major Arthur Godfrey Peuchen, starting to undress for the night, thought it was like a heavy wave striking the ship. Mrs. J. Stuart White was sitting on the edge of her bed, just reaching to turn out the light, when the ship seemed to roll over "a thousand marbles." To Lady Cosmo Duff Gordon, waking up from the jolt, it seemed "as though somebody had drawn a giant finger along the side of the ship." Mrs. John Jacob Astor thought it was some mishap in the kitchen.

20 It seemed stronger to some than to others. Mrs. Albert Caldwell pictured a large dog that had a baby kitten in its mouth and was shaking it. Mrs. Walter B. Stephenson recalled the first **ominous** jolt when she was in the San Francisco earthquake—then decided this wasn't that bad. Mrs. E. D. Appleton felt hardly any shock at all, but she noticed an unpleasant ripping sound . . . like someone tearing a long, long strip of calico.[5]

21 The jar meant more to J. Bruce Ismay, Managing Director of the White Star Line, who in a festive mood was going along for the ride on the *Titanic's* first trip. Ismay woke up with a start in his deluxe suite on B Deck—he felt sure the ship had struck something, but he didn't know what.

Excerpted from *A Night to Remember* by Walter Lord, published by Bantam Books.

---

5. **calico** a type of rough fabric of woven cotton with a printed pattern

✎ WRITE

PERSONAL RESPONSE: How do the reactions of the *Titanic* passengers affect your feelings, such as sympathy, about the collision? How does reading these personal reactions help you better understand what happened? Be sure to use evidence to support your response.

Address to the Nation on the Explosion of the Space Shuttle *Challenger*

INFORMATIONAL TEXT
Ronald Reagan
1986

Introduction

On January 28, 1986, millions of Americans watched on live TV as the Space Shuttle *Challenger* violently exploded just 73 seconds after takeoff, killing all seven people on board. It was the tenth mission for *Challenger*, but the first scheduled to carry an ordinary citizen into space, a teacher from New Hampshire named Christa McAuliffe. That evening, President Ronald Reagan (1911–2004) addressed the nation, including the many school children who witnessed the disaster, and lauded the bravery of the fallen crew.

"We're still pioneers. They, the members of the *Challenger* crew, were pioneers."

January 28, 1986

NOTES

1 Ladies and gentlemen, I'd planned to speak to you tonight to report on the state of the Union,[1] but the events of earlier today have led me to change those plans. Today is a day for mourning and remembering. Nancy and I are pained to the core by the tragedy of the shuttle *Challenger*. We know we share this pain with all of the people of our country. This is truly a national loss.

2 Nineteen years ago, almost to the day, we lost three astronauts in a terrible accident on the ground. But we've never lost an astronaut in flight; we've never had a tragedy like this. And perhaps we've forgotten the courage it took for the crew of the shuttle. But they, the *Challenger* Seven, were aware of the dangers, but overcame them and did their jobs brilliantly. We mourn seven heroes: Michael Smith, Dick Scobee, Judith Resnik, Ronald McNair, Ellison Onizuka, Gregory Jarvis, and Christa McAuliffe. We mourn their loss as a nation together.

Five astronauts and two payload specialists make up the STS 51-L crew, scheduled to fly aboard the Space Shuttle *Challenger* in January of 1986. Crew members are (left to right, front row) astronauts Michael J. Smith, Francis R. (Dick) Scobee, and Ronald E. McNair; and (left to right, back row) Ellison S. Onizuka, Sharon Christa McAuliffe, Gregory Jarvis, and Judith A. Resnik.

3 For the families of the seven, we cannot bear, as you do, the full impact of this tragedy. But we feel the loss, and we're thinking about you so very much. Your loved ones were daring and brave, and they had that special **grace,** that special spirit that says, "Give me a challenge, and I'll meet it with joy." They had a hunger to explore the universe and discover its truths. They wished to serve, and they did. They served all of us. We've grown used to wonders in

1. **State of the Union** Reagan had previously planned to deliver the State of the Union, an annual speech given by U.S. presidents before Congress on general topics

Skill:
Summarizing

Reagan calls members of the Challenger crew pioneers. Although we have become used to the idea of space, we must remember we are all still pioneers. The Challenger crew wished to serve and met the challenge with joy. We feel their loss.

Copyright © BookheadEd Learning, LLC

this century. It's hard to dazzle us. But for 25 years the United States space program has been doing just that. We've grown used to the idea of space, and perhaps we forget that we've only just begun. We're still pioneers. They, the members of the *Challenger* crew, were pioneers.

4   And I want to say something to the schoolchildren of America who were watching the live coverage of the shuttle's takeoff. I know it is hard to understand, but sometimes painful things like this happen. It's all part of the process of exploration and discovery. It's all part of taking a chance and expanding man's **horizons**. The future doesn't belong to the fainthearted; it belongs to the brave. The *Challenger* crew was pulling us into the future, and we'll continue to follow them.

5   I've always had great faith in and respect for our space program, and what happened today does nothing to diminish it. We don't hide our space program. We don't keep secrets and cover things up. We do it all up front and in public. That's the way freedom is, and we wouldn't change it for a minute. We'll continue our quest in space. There will be more shuttle flights and more shuttle crews and, yes, more volunteers, more civilians, more teachers in space. Nothing ends here; our hopes and our journeys continue. I want to add that I wish I could talk to every man and woman who works for NASA or who worked on this mission and tell them: "Your dedication and **professionalism** have moved and impressed us for decades. And we know of your **anguish.** We share it."

Skill:
Informational
Text Structure

In the second-to-last paragraph, Reagan mentions Sir Francis Drake. He was an ocean explorer who died at sea 390 years ago. Here Reagan uses a compare-and-contrast text structure to compare the Challenger crew to another explorer.

6   There's a **coincidence** today. On this day 390 years ago, the great explorer Sir Francis Drake died aboard ship off the coast of Panama. In his lifetime the great frontiers were the oceans, and an historian later said, "He lived by the sea, died on it, and was buried in it." Well, today we can say of the *Challenger* crew: Their dedication was, like Drake's, complete.

7   The crew of the space shuttle *Challenger* honored us by the manner in which they lived their lives. We will never forget them, nor the last time we saw them, this morning, as they prepared for their journey and waved goodbye and "slipped the surly bonds of earth" to "touch the face of God."

First Read

Read "Address to the Nation on the Explosion of the Space Shuttle *Challenger*." After you read, complete the Think Questions below.

☁ THINK QUESTIONS

1. Refer to one or more details from the text to support your understanding of the significance of the *Challenger* tragedy. What words and phrases in the first two paragraphs indicate this significance?

2. How does President Reagan describe the astronauts? Use details from the text to write two or three sentences that summarize his description.

3. Write two or three sentences explaining how President Reagan feels about the space program. What details does he offer to support his ideas? Cite evidence from the text to support your answer.

4. Use context to determine the meaning of the word **horizons** as it is used in this speech. Write your definition of *horizons* here and tell how you found it.

5. Remembering that the Latin prefix *co-* means "together," use the context clues provided in the passage to determine the meaning of **coincidence**. Write your definition of *coincidence* here and tell how you got it.

Please note that excerpts and passages in the StudySync® library and this workbook are intended as touchstones to generate interest in an author's work. The excerpts and passages do not substitute for the reading of entire texts, and StudySync® strongly recommends that students seek out and purchase the whole literary or informational work in order to experience it as the author intended. Links to online resellers are available in our digital library. In addition, complete works may be ordered through an authorized reseller by filling out and returning to StudySync® the order form enclosed in this workbook.

Reading & Writing Companion   **33**

SUMMARIZING

sync•skills

Skill:
Summarizing

Use the Checklist to analyze Summarizing in "Address to the Nation on the Explosion of the Space Shuttle *Challenger*." Refer to the sample student annotations about Summarizing in the text.

••• CHECKLIST FOR SUMMARIZING

In order to determine how to write an objective summary of a text, note the following:

✓ in a nonfiction text, examine the details, making notations in a notebook or graphic organizer

- ask basic questions such as *who, what, when, where, why,* and *how*
- identify what each of the details describe or have in common
- determine what central or main idea ties all the information together

✓ use the main idea as the topic sentence of the summary

✓ stay objective and do not add your own personal thoughts, judgments, or opinions to the summary

To provide an objective summary of a text, consider the following questions:

✓ What are the answers to basic *who, what, where, when, why,* and *how* questions in works of nonfiction?

✓ Have I determined what each of the details have in common and what central or main idea ties them together?

✓ In what order should I put the main ideas and most important details in a work of nonfiction to make my summary clear and logical?

✓ Is my summary objective, or have I added my own thoughts, judgments, and personal opinions?

Copyright © BookheadEd Learning, LLC

Skill: Summarizing

Reread paragraph 5 of "Address to the Nation on the Explosion of the Space Shuttle *Challenger*." Then, using the Checklist on the previous page, answer the multiple-choice questions below.

♻ YOUR TURN

1. This question has two parts. First, answer Part A. Then, answer Part B.

   Part A: What is the main idea of paragraph 5?

   ○ A. It is important to keep the space program hidden from the public.

   ○ B. NASA will continue with their space exploration program.

   ○ C. President Reagan wants to talk to everyone at NASA who worked on this mission.

   ○ D. More teachers will be in space one day.

   Part B: Which two details from the paragraph support your answer to Part A?

   ○ A. "We don't hide our space program" and "we know of your anguish."

   ○ B. "We don't hide our space program" and "we don't keep secrets and cover things up."

   ○ C. "There will be more shuttle flights and more shuttle crews and, yes, more volunteers, more civilians, more teachers in space" and "nothing ends here; our hopes and our journeys continue."

   ○ D. "We do it all up front and in public" and "we know of your anguish."

2. In paragraph 5, what is the important link between Reagan's statements about the space program and the people who work at NASA that supports the main idea and should be included in a summary?

   ○ A. President Reagan says that we don't hide our space program, and we don't keep secrets and cover things up.

   ○ B. Reagan states that there will be more shuttle flights and more shuttle crews, more volunteers, more civilians, and more teachers in space.

   ○ C. Reagan says that "our journeys continue," and this is supported by his statements that he has great faith in the space program, and that the professionalism and dedication of the people who work at NASA have impressed us for decades.

   ○ D. President Reagan says that he has to talk to every man and woman who works for NASA or this mission about hiding the space program so tragedies like *Challenger* do not happen again.

Skill:
Informational Text Structure

Use the Checklist to analyze Informational Text Structure in "Address to the Nation on the Explosion of the Space Shuttle *Challenger*." Refer to the sample student annotations about Informational Text Structure in the text.

••• CHECKLIST FOR INFORMATIONAL TEXT STRUCTURE

In order to determine the structure of a specific paragraph in a text, note the following:

✓ details and signal words that reveal the text structure in a paragraph of the text

✓ a key concept in the paragraph that is revealed by the text structure the author has chosen to organize the text

✓ particular sentences in the paragraph and the role they play in defining and refining a key concept

To analyze in detail the structure of a specific paragraph in a text, including the role of particular sentences in developing and refining a key concept, consider the following questions:

✓ What is the structure of the paragraph?

✓ Which sentences in the paragraph reveal the text structure the author is using?

✓ What role do these sentences play in developing and refining a key concept?

Skill:
Informational Text Structure

Reread paragraph 3 of "Address to the Nation on the Explosion of the Space Shuttle *Challenger*." Then, using the Checklist on the previous page, answer the multiple-choice questions below.

⟳ YOUR TURN

1. The primary text structure in paragraph 3 is—

   ○ A. description.
   ○ B. cause and effect.
   ○ C. problem and solution.
   ○ D. compare and contrast.

2. The author develops this text structure by—

   ○ A. using the word *but* to identify differences.
   ○ B. discussing change over time to describe a solution to a problem.
   ○ C. starting many of the clauses with similar phrases to describe or define the qualities of two groups.
   ○ D. describing two groups' feelings after the *Challenger* disaster to develop its effect.

3. This text structure helps develop the author's thesis by—

   ○ A. developing the key concept that the disaster was a great loss because the astronauts had families.
   ○ B. developing the key concept that the disaster was a great loss because it was the end result of decades of research.
   ○ C. developing the key concept that the disaster was a great loss because many Americans were saddened by the disaster.
   ○ D. developing the key concept that the disaster was a great loss because Americans lost a group of special people who were willing to take on an important challenge for their country.

Please note that excerpts and passages in the StudySync® library and this workbook are intended as touchstones to generate interest in an author's work. The excerpts and passages do not substitute for the reading of entire texts, and StudySync® strongly recommends that students seek out and purchase the whole literary or informational work in order to experience it as the author intended. Links to online resellers are available in our digital library. In addition, complete works may be ordered through an authorized reseller by filling out and returning to StudySync® the order form enclosed in this workbook.

Reading & Writing Companion   37

Close Read

Reread "Address to the Nation on the Explosion of the Space Shuttle *Challenger*." As you reread, complete the Skills Focus questions below. Then use your answers and annotations from the questions to help you complete the Write activity.

◎ SKILLS FOCUS

1. Identify examples of compare-and-contrast structure in the text. Explain how these comparisons help develop the thesis, or central message, in Reagan's speech.

2. Identify Reagan's stance on the space program. Write one or two sentences summarizing his message.

3. Identify details in the text that show the risks of the space program. Explain why astronauts are willing to take chances and explore space.

✎ WRITE

COMPARE AND CONTRAST: In "Address to the Nation on the Explosion of the Space Shuttle *Challenger*," President Reagan addresses the public about a national tragedy. In *A Night to Remember*, the tragedy is recounted through interviews with various people who experienced the *Titanic's* crash. How do the different structures of the texts help to effectively communicate information regarding the tragedies? Are there advantages or disadvantages to the structure of either text? Which one do you prefer? Cite specific examples from the text to explain which structure better helps to effectively communicate information and make the author's point.

A Kenyan Teen's Discovery:

Let There Be Lights to Save Lions

INFORMATIONAL TEXT
Nina Gregory
2013

Introduction

Having roamed the lands of present-day Kenya and Tanzania for thousands of years, the Maasai tribe had long coexisted with the region's lion population. But now, the lion population is in sharp decline—and their next-door neighbors are a big reason why. Richard Turere is one of those neighbors, a 13-year-old inventor who lives among the Maasai near Nairobi National Park, which hosts many of the endangered lions of Kenya. Living in such close proximity, some lions have begun to prey on the livestock owned by locals like Richard's family. A struggle has emerged between the locals and the encroaching lions, resulting in deaths of a highly threatened and endangered species (there are fewer than 2,000 lions remaining in Kenya). In this article and its accompanying video, explore how young Richard devised an inventive way to save both livestock and lions from harm

"A light went on inside him and an idea was born."

1   One of the talks from the TED stage in Long Beach, Calif., this week came from Richard Turere, an inventor. He is a Maasai from Kenya. And he's 13.

2   "From ages 6 to 9, I started looking after my father's cows," Richard says. "I'd take them out in the morning and bring them back in the evening. We put them in a small cow shed at night," and that's when the trouble would start. Lions would jump in the shed and kill the cows, which are enclosed and an easy target.

3   Lions are the top tourist attraction to Kenya, especially in the Nairobi National Park, which is near where Richard lives. Lions are also considered **critically** endangered in Kenya.

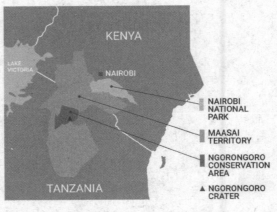

Map showing Maasai Territory, Nairobi National Park area, Ngorongoro Conservation Area, and Ngorongoro Crater.*
*Approximate sizes of areas and locations.

Skill: Media

According to the video I saw, killing lions can also be cultural. However, this seems to be the bigger problem. The article and the video showing the lions and livestock offer a variety of ways to understand why Richard's invention is so important.

4   The Kenya Wildlife Service estimates there are just 2,000 lions left in the country. One of the main causes of their demise, "is that people kill them in **retaliation** for lions attacking their livestock," says Paula Kahumbu, executive director of Wildlife Direct, a wildlife **conservation** organization in Africa.

NOTES

5   She has been studying the **conflict** between humans and lions, and her work led her to Richard. In one week, she **monitored** over 50 cases where lions attacked livestock. "It's a very, very serious problem," she says.

6   Her work studying the problem led her to Richard.

7   One night he was walking around with a flashlight and discovered the lions were scared of a moving light. A light went on inside him and an idea was born.

8   Three weeks and much tinkering later, Richard had invented a system of lights that flash around the cow shed, **mimicking** a human walking around with a flashlight. His system is made from broken flashlight parts and an indicator box from a motorcycle.

9   "The only thing I bought was a solar panel," which charges a battery that supplies power to the lights at night, Richard says. He calls the system Lion Lights.

10 "There have been a lot of efforts to try to protect the lions," Kahumbu says. "It's a crisis and everyone is looking for a solution. One idea was land leases, another was lion-proof fences. And basically no one even knew that Richard had already come up with something that worked."

11 His simple solution was so successful, his neighbors heard about it and wanted Lion Lights, too. He installed the lights for them and for six other homes in his community. From there, the lights spread and are now being used all around Kenya. Someone in India is trying them out for tigers. In Zambia and Tanzania they're being used, as well.

12 To get to the TED stage, Richard traveled on an airplane for the first time in his life. He says he has a lot to tell his friends about when he goes back home, and among the scholars and prize winners, scientists and poets, what impressed him the most on his trip was something he saw at the nearby Aquarium of the Pacific: "It was my first time seeing a shark. I've never seen a shark."

Skill:
Word Patterns and
Relationships

Kahumbu says protecting lions is a crisis and everyone is looking for a solution. An antonym for solution is problem. But this seems like more than just a problem as there have been so many efforts to solve it. So, a crisis must mean an emergency.

Please note that excerpts and passages in the StudySync® library and this workbook are intended as touchstones to generate interest in an author's work. The excerpts and passages do not substitute for the reading of entire texts, and StudySync® strongly recommends that students seek out and purchase the whole literary or informational work in order to experience it as the author intended. Links to online resellers are available in our digital library. In addition, complete works may be ordered through an authorized reseller by filling out and returning to StudySync® the order form enclosed in this workbook.

Reading & Writing
Companion

41

First Read

Read "A Kenyan Teen's Discovery: Let There Be Lights to Save Lions." After you read, complete the Think Questions below.

☁ THINK QUESTIONS

1. Why does Richard's invention work so well? How does it keep the lions away from the livestock without harming them? Use specific evidence from the text to support your answer.

2. What items did Richard use to create his invention? Did he have to buy a lot of expensive equipment? Why or why not?

3. Before Richard's idea became known, what were some of the other ideas people had to keep the lions from attacking livestock? Cite specific examples from the text.

4. The root *serv* comes from the Latin word *servare*, meaning "to save or guard." With this in mind, write a definition of **conservation** in your own words, indicating any words or phrases that helped you understand.

5. Use context clues to find the meaning of the word **retaliation** as it is used in paragraph 4. Write your own definition of *retaliation*, identifying any context clues that helped you unlock the meaning of the word.

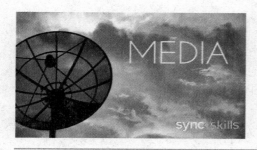

Skill:
Media

Use the Checklist to analyze Media in "A Kenyan Teen's Discovery: Let There Be Lights to Save Lions." Refer to the sample student annotations about Media in the text.

••• CHECKLIST FOR MEDIA

In order to identify the purpose of information and the advantages and disadvantages of presenting it in different forms of media, note the following:

- ✓ the features of each medium, such as print or digital text, video, and multimedia

- ✓ how the medium contributes to the information in the text

- ✓ how the same information can be treated, or presented, in more than one medium, including visually, quantitatively, or orally

- ✓ how different media present a particular topic, idea, or historical event and can include diaries, eyewitness accounts, films, books, news and feature articles, or photographs

- ✓ which details are emphasized or absent in each medium and the reasons behind these choices

- ✓ how readers and historians compare and contrast accounts in different media as they analyze and interpret events

- ✓ the reliability of each medium, including specific words and images that can help you identify the motive or motives behind a video, oral, quantitative, or written work

To evaluate the advantages and disadvantages of using different media to present a particular topic or idea and analyze the purpose of presenting information in diverse formats, ask the following questions:

- ✓ What are the advantages and disadvantages of using different media to present a particular topic or idea?

- ✓ What was the purpose behind the creation of this video, speech, book, or article?

- ✓ What were the motives behind its presentation? How do you know?

Skill:
Media

Watch the video clips from "Inside Africa" on the StudySync site as indicated for each question. Then, using the Checklist on the previous page, answer the multiple-choice questions below.

⟳ YOUR TURN

1. Watch from the beginning of the video to 00:24. Both types of media—video and audio—of the Maasai man and his herd are intended to—

   ○ A. provide background information about Maasai life.
   ○ B. emphasize threats to cattle in the region.
   ○ C. show that the cattle suffer during seasonal changes.
   ○ D. show the distance the cattle travel.

2. Watch the video from 03:47 to 04:13. The interaction of visual and audio in the video clip in the explanation of the lion-killing ritual is intended to—

   ○ A. suggest that lion hunting is dangerous.
   ○ B. show that it is difficult to kill a lion.
   ○ C. emphasize the symbolic importance of the ritual.
   ○ D. explain why the ritual has been outlawed in the region.

3. The main advantage of using both digital text and the video clip is to make sure that the reader—

   ○ A. knows where the region is located and what the land looks like.
   ○ B. is provided with background knowledge about Kenyan culture.
   ○ C. understands the key ideas of the lion problem and its solution.
   ○ D. grasps how Richard Turere's invention works.

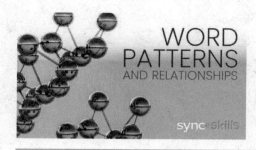

Skill: Word Patterns and Relationships

Use the Checklist to analyze Word Patterns and Relationships in "A Kenyan Teen's Discovery: Let There Be Lights to Save Lions." Refer to the sample student annotations about Word Patterns and Relationships in the text.

••• CHECKLIST FOR WORD PATTERNS AND RELATIONSHIPS

In order to determine the relationship between specific words to better understand each one, note the following:

- ✓ any unfamiliar words in the text

- ✓ surrounding words and phrases to better understand word meanings or any possible relationships between words

- ✓ examples of part/whole, item/category, or other relationships between words, such as cause/effect, analogies, or synonym/antonym relationships

- ✓ ways that the specific words relate to each other

To analyze the relationship between specific words to better understand each one, consider the following questions:

- ✓ Are these words related to each other in some way? How?

- ✓ What kind of relationship do these words have?

- ✓ How can I use the relationship between two or more specific words to better understand each of the words?

- ✓ Can any of these words be defined by identifying a synonym/antonym or cause/effect relationship?

Please note that excerpts and passages in the StudySync® library and this workbook are intended as touchstones to generate interest in an author's work. The excerpts and passages do not substitute for the reading of entire texts, and StudySync® strongly recommends that students seek out and purchase the whole literary or informational work in order to experience it as the author intended. Links to online resellers are available in our digital library. In addition, complete works may be ordered through an authorized reseller by filling out and returning to StudySync® the order form enclosed in this workbook.

Reading & Writing Companion   45

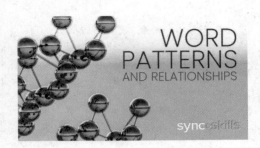

Skill: Word Patterns and Relationships

Reread paragraphs 5–9 of "A Kenyan Teen's Discovery: Let There Be Lights to Save Lions." Then, using the Checklist on the previous page, answer the multiple-choice questions below.

↻ YOUR TURN

1. The word *light* appears twice in paragraph 7. How is the meaning of the word in the first sentence different from the way the word is used in the second sentence of the paragraph?

   ○ A. In the first sentence the world *light* means "something that is moving," and in the second sentence it refers to the beginnings of an idea.

   ○ B. In the first sentence the word *light* means "illumination that makes things visible," and in the second sentence it refers to Richard shining the flashlight on himself.

   ○ C. In the first sentence the word *light* means "illumination that makes things visible," and in the second sentence it refers to the beginnings of an idea.

   ○ D. In the first sentence the word *light* means "something that comes out of a flashlight," and in the second sentence it refers to the beginnings of an idea.

2. How does the relationship between the two meanings of the word *light* help you to better understand how the author uses the word to create and highlight meaning in the text?

   ○ A. The first meaning of the word *light* helps Richard to make a discovery about the lions and their behavior because he is using a flashlight. The meaning of the word in the second sentence refers to the idea that Richard had to solve a problem.

   ○ B. The meanings of the word *light* and the way they are used are related because in the first sentence, *light* means actual illumination that Richard uses to see the lions in the darkness. In the second sentence it means the light Richard uses to see something within himself.

   ○ C. The meanings are related because one refers to the flashlight Richard uses while walking around at night, and the other indicates that Richard has a light within him, or an idea, to help him "see" a solution to his problem.

   ○ D. The meaning of the word *light* and the way the word is used in the first and second sentences are related. In the first sentence it means the actual illumination that makes things visible. In the second sentence it is used in a symbolic way to refer to a sudden idea. While not an actual light, it indicates that Richard has a light within him, or an idea, to help him "see" a solution.

Close Read

Reread "A Kenyan Teen's Discovery: Let There Be Lights to Save Lions" and rewatch the video "Inside Africa" on the StudySync site. As you reread, complete the Skills Focus questions below. Then use your answers and annotations from the questions to help you complete the Write activity.

◎ SKILLS FOCUS

1. Identify a detail from the article that is clarified by the map. Explain the advantage of including the map to convey information.

2. Identify evidence that shows how Richard Turere's invention works. Write a two-sentence summary of his process.

3. Identify a detail from the article that is developed by the video. Explain the advantage of including the video to understand this information.

4. How and why did Richard Turere take a chance with the creation of his invention? What was risky about this venture? How did his invention impact his community once it was introduced?

✎ WRITE

INFORMATIVE: How do the video and the text work together to introduce and explain the impact of Richard Turere's invention? What are the advantages and disadvantages of using these different media in the article? Cite evidence from both the text and the video in your response.

Please note that excerpts and passages in the StudySync® library and this workbook are intended as touchstones to generate interest in an author's work. The excerpts and passages do not substitute for the reading of entire texts, and StudySync® strongly recommends that students seek out and purchase the whole literary or informational work in order to experience it as the author intended. Links to online resellers are available in our digital library. In addition, complete works may be ordered through an authorized reseller by filling out and returning to StudySync® the order form enclosed in this workbook.

Reading & Writing Companion   47

Mother to Son

POETRY
Langston Hughes
1922

Introduction

African American poet Langston Hughes (1902–1967) is one of the best-known poets of the Harlem Renaissance, a cultural and intellectual movement that began in the 1920s and resulted in the production of African American literature, art, and music that challenged racism and promoted progressive politics, such as racial and social integration. In Hughes's poem "Mother to Son," the speaker is a mother who draws on her own experiences to teach her son about perseverance.

"Well, son, I'll tell you: Life for me ain't been no crystal stair."

1 Well, son, I'll tell you:
2 Life for me ain't been no **crystal** stair.
3 It's had tacks in it,
4 And **splinters,**
5 And boards torn up,
6 And places with no carpet on the floor—
7 Bare.
8 But all the time
9 I'se been a-climbin' on,
10 And reachin' **landin's,**
11 And turnin' corners,
12 And sometimes goin' in the dark
13 Where there ain't been no light.
14 So, boy, don't you turn back.
15 Don't you set down on the steps
16 'Cause you finds it's kinder hard.
17 Don't you fall now—
18 For I'se still goin', honey,
19 I'se still climbin',
20 And life for me ain't been no crystal stair.

Please note that excerpts and passages in the StudySync® library and this workbook are intended as touchstones to generate interest in an author's work. The excerpts and passages do not substitute for the reading of entire texts, and StudySync® strongly recommends that students seek out and purchase the whole literary or informational work in order to experience it as the author intended. Links to online resellers are available in our digital library. In addition, complete works may be ordered through an authorized reseller by filling out and returning to StudySync® the order form enclosed in this workbook.

Reading & Writing Companion

49

WRITE

PERSONAL RESPONSE: The mother of the poem's title shows sympathy for her son, but she does not let him dwell on defeat. What did you think about the mother's advice in "Mother to Son"? What kind of advice have you received from an adult in your life? What kind of a metaphor could you use to share the advice with a friend?

Learning to Read

POETRY
Frances Ellen Watkins Harper
1854

Introduction

Born a free woman in Baltimore, Frances Ellen Watkins Harper (1825–1911) is known by some as the mother of African American journalism. Harper experienced commercial success as a poet and novelist, and she is credited with establishing the tradition of African American protest poetry. Harper also helped enslaved people escape along the Underground Railroad and was a well-known public speaker and civil rights activist. In the poem "Learning to Read," she animates her real-life experiences talking to newly-freed enslaved people. "Learning to Read" is told from the perspective of a woman who fights to earn her education late in life.

"Knowledge didn't agree with slavery—
'Twould make us all too wise."

NOTES

1   Very soon the **Yankee** teachers
2   Came down and set up school;
3   But, oh! how the **Rebs** did hate it,—
4   It was agin' their rule.

5   Our masters always tried to hide
6   Book learning from our eyes;
7   Knowledge didn't agree with slavery—
8   'Twould make us all too wise.

9   But some of us would try to steal
10   A little from the book.
11   And put the words together,
12   And learn by **hook or crook**.

13   I remember Uncle Caldwell,
14   Who took pot liquor fat
15   And greased the pages of his book,
16   And hid it in his hat.

17   And had his master ever seen
18   The **leaves** upon his head,
19   He'd have thought them greasy papers,
20   But nothing to be read.

21   And there was Mr. Turner's Ben,
22   Who heard the children spell,
23   And picked the words right up by heart,
24   And learned to read 'em well.

25   Well, the Northern folks kept sending
26   The Yankee teachers down;
27   And they stood right up and helped us,
28   Though Rebs did **sneer** and frown.

29 And I longed to read my Bible,
30   For precious words it said;
31 But when I begun to learn it,
32   Folks just shook their heads,

33 And said there is no use trying,
34   Oh! Chloe, you're too late;
35 But as I was rising sixty,
36   I had no time to wait.

37 So I got a pair of glasses,
38   And straight to work I went,
39 And never stopped till I could read
40   The hymns and Testament.[1]

41 Then I got a little cabin
42   A place to call my own—
43 And I felt independent
44   As the queen upon her throne.

Frances Harper (1825–1911), African-American poet, abolitionist, novelist, lecturer, and womens rights advocate

---

1. **Testament** the Christian Bible is split into two Testaments, Old and New

---

✏️ WRITE

DISCUSSION: It's often said that "knowledge is power." The speaker of the poem presents the reason enslaved people were not allowed to learn to read: "Knowledge didn't agree with slavery— / 'Twould make us all too wise." Discuss these ideas and your response to the poem.

Please note that excerpts and passages in the StudySync® library and this workbook are intended as touchstones to generate interest in an author's work. The excerpts and passages do not substitute for the reading of entire texts, and StudySync® strongly recommends that students seek out and purchase the whole literary or informational work in order to experience it as the author intended. Links to online resellers are available in our digital library. In addition, complete works may be ordered through an authorized reseller by filling out and returning to StudySync® the order form enclosed in this workbook.

Reading & Writing Companion   53

Narrative of the Life of Frederick Douglass, An American Slave

INFORMATIONAL TEXT
Frederick Douglass
1845

Introduction

P ublished in 1845, *Narrative of the Life of Frederick Douglass, An American Slave* describes Douglass's journey from slavery to freedom. This great American orator provides a factual account of his struggle to educate and free himself and others from the oppression of his times. The memoir's vivid descriptions of life as an enslaved person played a key role in fueling the abolitionist movement in the North prior to the Civil War. In the following excerpt from the middle of the text, Douglass (ca. 1818–1895) overcomes the odds against him, procuring the assistance of others in teaching himself to read despite laws prohibiting slaves from

"The silver trump of freedom had roused my soul to eternal wakefulness."

from Chapter VII

NOTES

1   I lived in Master Hugh's family about seven years. During this time, I succeeded in learning to read and write. In accomplishing this, I was compelled to resort to various stratagems.[1] I had no regular teacher. My mistress, who had kindly commenced to instruct me, had, in compliance with the advice and direction of her husband, not only ceased to instruct, but had set her face against my being instructed by any one else. It is due, however, to my mistress to say of her, that she did not adopt this course of treatment immediately. She at first lacked the depravity indispensable to shutting me up in mental darkness. It was at least necessary for her to have some training in the exercise of irresponsible power, to make her equal to the task of treating me as though I were a brute.

2   My mistress was, as I have said, a kind and tender-hearted woman; and in the simplicity of her soul she commenced, when I first went to live with her, to treat me as she supposed one human being ought to treat another. In entering upon the duties of a slaveholder, she did not seem to perceive that I sustained to her the relation of a mere chattel, and that for her to treat me as a human being was not only wrong, but dangerously so. Slavery proved as injurious to her as it did to me. When I went there, she was a pious, warm, and tender-hearted woman. There was no sorrow or suffering for which she had not a tear. She had bread for the hungry, clothes for the naked, and comfort for every mourner that came within her reach. Slavery soon proved its ability to divest her of these heavenly qualities. Under its influence, the tender heart became stone, and the lamblike disposition gave way to one of tiger-like fierceness. The first step in her downward course was in her ceasing to instruct me. She now commenced to practise her husband's precepts. She finally became even more violent in her opposition than her husband himself. She was not satisfied with simply doing as well as he had commanded; she seemed anxious to do better. Nothing seemed to make her more angry than to see me with a newspaper. She seemed to think that here lay the danger. I have had her rush at me with a face made all up of fury, and snatch from me a newspaper, in a manner that fully revealed her apprehension. She was an

Skill:
Figurative
Language

A lamb and a tiger remind me of the lamb and the lion in the Bible. The allusion continues as Douglass describes how his mistress changes from having kind and generous qualities to having a hardened heart and the fierceness of a tiger.

---

1. **stratagems** a plan or strategy to trick an enemy or achieve a goal

NOTES

apt woman; and a little experience soon demonstrated, to her satisfaction, that education and slavery were incompatible with each other.

3   From this time I was most narrowly watched. If I was in a separate room any considerable length of time, I was sure to be suspected of having a book, and was at once called to give an account of myself. All this, however, was too late. The first step had been taken. Mistress, in teaching me the alphabet, had given me the *inch,* and no precaution could prevent me from taking the ell.[2]

Skill: Informational Text Elements

Earlier in the text, Douglass's mistress refused to teach him anymore, so he had to find another way to learn to read. The mistress became cruel, but these white boys are helpful. The white boys and the mistress are connected because they are key to Douglass's ability to read.

4   The plan which I adopted, and the one by which I was most successful, was that of making friends of all the little white boys whom I met in the street. As many of these as I could, I converted into teachers. With their kindly aid, obtained at different times and in different places, I finally succeeded in learning to read. When I was sent of errands, I always took my book with me, and by going one part of my errand quickly, I found time to get a lesson before my return. I used also to carry bread with me, enough of which was always in the house, and to which I was always welcome; for I was much better off in this regard than many of the poor white children in our neighborhood. This bread I used to **bestow** upon the hungry little urchins, who, in return, would give me that more valuable bread of knowledge. I am strongly tempted to give the names of two or three of those little boys, as a testimonial of the gratitude and affection I bear them; but **prudence** forbids;— not that it would injure me, but it might embarrass them; for it is almost an unpardonable offence to teach slaves to read in this Christian country. It is enough to say of the dear little fellows, that they lived on Philpot Street, very near Durgin and Bailey's ship-yard. I used to talk this matter of slavery over with them. I would sometimes say to them, I wished I could be as free as they would be when they got to be men. "You will be free as soon as you are twenty-one, but I am a slave for life! Have not I as good a right to be free as you have?" These words used to trouble them; they would express for me the liveliest sympathy, and **console** me with the hope that something would occur by which I might be free.

5   I was now about twelve years old, and the thought of being a slave for life began to **bear** heavily upon my heart. Just about this time, I got hold of a book entitled "The Columbian Orator." Every opportunity I got, I used to read this book. Among much of other interesting matter, I found in it a dialogue between a master and his slave. The slave was represented as having run away from his master three times. The dialogue represented the conversation which took place between them, when the slave was retaken the third time. In this dialogue, the whole argument in behalf of slavery was brought forward by the master, all of which was disposed of by the slave. The slave was made to say some very smart as well as impressive things in reply to his

––––––––––––
2. *ell* (archaic) a six hand-width measurement used in textile-making

master—things which had the desired though unexpected effect; for the conversation resulted in the voluntary emancipation of the slave on the part of the master.

6 In the same book, I met with one of Sheridan's mighty speeches on and in behalf of Catholic emancipation. These were choice documents to me. I read them over and over again with unabated interest. They gave tongue to interesting thoughts of my own soul, which had frequently flashed through my mind, and died away for want of utterance. The moral which I gained from the dialogue was the power of truth over the conscience of even a slaveholder. What I got from Sheridan was a bold denunciation of slavery, and a powerful vindication of human rights.

7 The reading of these documents enabled me to utter my thoughts, and to meet the arguments brought forward to sustain slavery; but while they relieved me of one difficulty, they brought on another even more painful than the one of which I was relieved. The more I read, the more I was led to abhor and detest my enslavers. I could regard them in no other light than a band of successful robbers, who had left their homes, and gone to Africa, and stolen us from our homes, and in a strange land reduced us to slavery. I loathed them as being the meanest as well as the most wicked of men. As I read and contemplated the subject, behold! that very discontentment which Master Hugh had predicted would follow my learning to read had already come, to torment and sting my soul to unutterable **anguish.** As I writhed under it, I would at times feel that learning to read had been a curse rather than a blessing. It had given me a view of my wretched condition, without the remedy. It opened my eyes to the horrible pit, but to no ladder upon which to get out. In moments of agony, I envied my fellow-slaves for their stupidity. I have often wished myself a beast. I preferred the condition of the meanest reptile to my own. Any thing, no matter what, to get rid of thinking! It was this everlasting thinking of my condition that tormented me. There was no getting rid of it. It was pressed upon me by every object within sight or hearing, animate or inanimate. The silver trump of freedom had roused my soul to eternal wakefulness. Freedom now appeared, to disappear no more forever. It was heard in every sound, and seen in every thing. It was ever present to torment me with a sense of my wretched condition. I saw nothing without seeing it, I heard nothing without hearing it, and felt nothing without feeling it. It looked from every star, it smiled in every calm, breathed in every wind, and moved in every storm.

8 I often found myself regretting my own existence, and wishing myself dead; and but for the hope of being free, I have no doubt but that I should have killed myself, or done something for which I should have been killed. While in this state of mind, I was eager to hear any one speak of slavery. I was a ready listener. Every little while, I could hear something about the abolitionists. It

was some time before I found what the word meant. It was always used in such connections as to make it an interesting word to me. If a slave ran away and succeeded in getting clear, or if a slave killed his master, set fire to a barn, or did any thing very wrong in the mind of a slaveholder, it was spoken of as the fruit of *abolition*. Hearing the word in this connection very often, I set about learning what it meant. The

American orator, editor, author, abolitionist, and former enslaved person Frederick Douglass (1818–1895) edits a journal at his desk, late 1870s.

dictionary afforded me little or no help. I found it was "the act of abolishing;" but then I did not know what was to be abolished. Here I was perplexed. I did not dare to ask any one about its meaning, for I was satisfied that it was something they wanted me to know very little about. After a patient waiting, I got one of our city papers, containing an account of the number of petitions from the north, praying for the abolition of slavery in the District of Columbia, and of the slave trade between the States. From this time I understood the words *abolition* and *abolitionist,* and always drew near when that word was spoken, expecting to hear something of importance to myself and fellow-slaves. The light broke in upon me by degrees. I went one day down on the wharf of Mr. Waters; and seeing two Irishmen unloading a scow of stone, I went, unasked, and helped them. When we had finished, one of them came to me and asked me if I were a slave. I told him I was. He asked, "Are ye a slave for life?" I told him that I was. The good Irishman seemed to be deeply affected by the statement. He said to the other that it was a pity so fine a little fellow as myself should be a slave for life. He said it was a shame to hold me. They both advised me to run away to the north; that I should find friends there, and that I should be free. I pretended not to be interested in what they said, and treated them as if I did not understand them; for I feared they might be treacherous. White men have been known to encourage slaves to escape, and then, to get the reward, catch them and return them to their masters. I was afraid that these seemingly good men might use me so; but I nevertheless remembered their advice, and from that time I resolved to run away. I looked forward to a time at which it would be safe for me to escape. I was too young to think of doing so immediately; besides, I wished to learn how to write, as I might have occasion to write my own pass. I consoled myself with the hope that I should one day find a good chance. Meanwhile, I would learn to write.

9 The idea as to how I might learn to write was suggested to me by being in Durgin and Bailey's ship-yard, and frequently seeing the ship carpenters, after hewing, and getting a piece of timber ready for use, write on the timber the name of that part of the ship for which it was intended. When a piece of timber was intended for the larboard side, it would be marked thus—"L."

When a piece was for the starboard side, it would be marked thus—"S." A piece for the larboard side forward, would be marked thus—"L. F." When a piece was for starboard side forward, it would be marked thus—"S. F." For larboard aft, it would be marked thus—"L. A." For starboard aft, it would be marked thus—"S. A." I soon learned the names of these letters, and for what they were intended when placed upon a piece of timber in the ship-yard. I immediately commenced copying them, and in a short time was able to make the four letters named. After that, when I met with any boy who I knew could write, I would tell him I could write as well as he. The next word would be, "I don't believe you. Let me see you try it." I would then make the letters which I had been so fortunate as to learn, and ask him to beat that. In this way I got a good many lessons in writing, which it is quite possible I should never have gotten in any other way. During this time, my copy-book was the board fence, brick wall, and pavement; my pen and ink was a lump of chalk. With these, I learned mainly how to write. I then commenced and continued copying the Italics in Webster's Spelling Book, until I could make them all without looking on the book. By this time, my little Master Thomas had gone to school, and learned how to write, and had written over a number of copy-books. These had been brought home, and shown to some of our near neighbors, and then laid aside. My mistress used to go to class meeting at the Wilk Street meetinghouse every Monday afternoon, and leave me to take care of the house. When left thus, I used to spend the time in writing in the spaces left in Master Thomas's copy-book, copying what he had written. I continued to do this until I could write a hand very similar to that of Master Thomas. Thus, after a long, tedious effort for years, I finally succeeded in learning how to write.

Please note that excerpts and passages in the StudySync® library and this workbook are intended as touchstones to generate interest in an author's work. The excerpts and passages do not substitute for the reading of entire texts, and StudySync® strongly recommends that students seek out and purchase the whole literary or informational work in order to experience it as the author intended. Links to online resellers are available in our digital library. In addition, complete works may be ordered through an authorized reseller by filling out and returning to StudySync® the order form enclosed in this workbook.

Reading & Writing
Companion

59

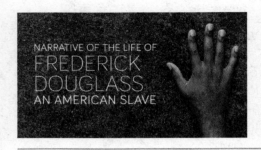

First Read

Read *Narrative of the Life of Frederick Douglass, An American Slave*. After you read, complete the Think Questions below.

☁ THINK QUESTIONS

1. Identify evidence from the excerpt that reveals why learning to read was so important to Frederick Douglass when he was a boy.

2. How did Douglass learn to read? Describe how he was affected by the texts he read.

3. Over time, Douglass begins to think that "learning to read had been a curse rather than a blessing." Why does he come to feel this way? Explain, citing evidence from the excerpt.

4. Based on context clues, what is the meaning of the word **console** as it is used in paragraph 4? Write your best definition of *console* here, explaining how you figured it out.

5. Read the following dictionary entry:

   bear
   bear \ber\ *verb*

   a. to carry
   b. to bring forth or produce
   c. to endure
   d. to weigh on or burden

   Which definition most closely matches the meaning of **bear** as it is used in paragraph 5? Write the correct definition of *bear* here and explain how you figured out the correct meaning.

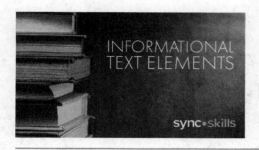

Skill:
Informational Text Elements

Use the Checklist to analyze Informational Text Elements in *Narrative of the Life of Frederick Douglass, An American Slave*. Refer to the sample student annotations about Informational Text Elements in the text.

••• CHECKLIST FOR INFORMATIONAL TEXT ELEMENTS

In order to determine how a text makes connections among and distinctions between individuals, ideas, or events, note the following:

✓ key details in the text that describe or explain important ideas, events, or individuals

✓ connections as well as distinctions between different individuals, ideas, and events, such as:

- particular characteristics
- shared experiences
- similar or different ideas
- important conversations

✓ analogies the author uses to determine the similarities between two pieces of information (e.g., a heart and a pump)

✓ comparisons the author makes between individuals, ideas, or events

To analyze how a text makes connections among and distinctions between individuals, ideas, or events, consider the following questions:

✓ What kinds of connections and distinctions does the author make in the text?

✓ Does the author include any analogies or comparisons? What do they add to the text?

✓ What other features, if any, help readers to analyze the events, ideas, or individuals in the text?

Skill:
Informational Text Elements

sync•skills

Reread paragraphs 5 and 6 of *Narrative of the Life of Frederick Douglass, An American Slave*. Then, using the Checklist on the previous page, answer the multiple-choice questions below.

🗘 YOUR TURN

1. According to the information in paragraph 5, why was discovering the *The Columbian Orator* important to Douglass?

   ○ A. Douglass enjoyed reading and could read this book often.

   ○ B. Douglass wanted to be free, and reading helped him feel free.

   ○ C. Douglass felt that he would always be an enslaved person, but this text gave him hope.

   ○ D. Douglass felt that he would always be an enslaved person, and this text presented a similar fate for another enslaved person.

2. Which detail from paragraph 6 best supports the idea that discovering *The Columbian Orator* was a key event in Douglass's life?

   ○ A. "In the same book, I met with one of Sheridan's mighty speeches on and in behalf of Catholic emancipation."

   ○ B. "These were choice documents to me. I read them over and over again with unabated interest."

   ○ C. "They gave tongue to interesting thoughts of my own soul, which had frequently flashed through my mind, and died away for want of utterance."

   ○ D. "What I got from Sheridan was a bold denunciation of slavery, and a powerful vindication of human rights."

3. What connection does Douglass make between the ideas in *The Columbian Orator* and his own situation?

   ○ A. Douglass realizes that he is just like the enslaved person in the book.

   ○ B. Douglass realizes that like the enslaved person in the book, he could use the power of the truth to gain his own freedom.

   ○ C. Douglass realizes that he is like the enslaved person in the book, but he will never be free.

   ○ D. Douglass realizes that human rights are important.

Skill:
Figurative Language

Use the Checklist to analyze Figurative Language in *Narrative of the Life of Frederick Douglass, An American Slave*. Refer to the sample student annotations about Figurative Language in the text.

••• CHECKLIST FOR FIGURATIVE LANGUAGE

To determine the meanings of figures of speech in a text, note the following:

✓ words that mean one thing literally and suggest something else

✓ similes, such as "strong as an ox"

✓ metaphors, such as "her eyes were stars"

✓ allusions, or indirect references to people, texts, events, or ideas, such as

- saying of a setting, "the place was a Garden of Eden" (biblical allusion)
- saying of a character whose snooping caused problems, "he opened a Pandora's box" (allusion to mythology)
- calling someone who likes romance "a real Romeo" (allusion to Shakespeare)

✓ verbal irony, or people saying one thing and meaning another, such as

- referring to a stormy day as "beautiful weather"
- a character saying how happy he is to be somewhere when he is not

✓ analogies, or comparisons of two unlike things based on a specific similarity and used for clarification, such as

- remarking, "Life is like a ball game; anybody can have a losing day."
- in Shakespeare's Sonnet 18, "Shall I compare thee to a summer's day? / Thou art more lovely and more temperate."

✓ other language in the text used in a nonliteral way

Please note that excerpts and passages in the StudySync® library and this workbook are intended as touchstones to generate interest in an author's work. The excerpts and passages do not substitute for the reading of entire texts, and StudySync® strongly recommends that students seek out and purchase the whole literary or informational work in order to experience it as the author intended. Links to online resellers are available in our digital library. In addition, complete works may be ordered through an authorized reseller by filling out and returning to StudySync® the order form enclosed in this workbook.

Reading & Writing Companion   **63**

In order to interpret the meaning of a figure of speech in context, ask the following questions:

- ✓ Does any of the descriptive language in the text compare two seemingly unlike things?

- ✓ Do any descriptions include *like* or *as,* indicating a simile?

- ✓ Is there a direct comparison that suggests a metaphor?

- ✓ What literary, biblical, or mythological allusions do you recognize?

- ✓ Can you detect humor or sarcasm in the tone of the word or phrase, or a character saying one thing and clearly meaning the opposite?

- ✓ How does the use of this figure of speech change your understanding of the thing or person being described?

In order to analyze the impact of figurative language on the meaning of a text, use the following questions as a guide:

- ✓ Where does figurative language appear in the text? What does it mean?

- ✓ Why does the author use figurative language rather than literal language?

Skill:
Figurative Language

Reread paragraph 4 of *Narrative of the Life of Frederick Douglass, An American Slave*. Then, using the Checklist on the previous page, answer the multiple-choice questions below.

↻ YOUR TURN

1. In paragraph 4, how does Douglass show his feelings for America?

   ○ A. He literally calls it a "Christian country," which means he likes it and thinks enslaved people shouldn't be taught to read.

   ○ B. He seems to sarcastically refer to it as a "Christian country," which shows that he doesn't think he should be taught to read.

   ○ C. He literally calls it a "Christian country," which shows that he doesn't like it very much.

   ○ D. He seems to sarcastically refer to it as a "Christian country," which shows that he doesn't like it because slavery exists and teaching enslaved people to read is not allowed.

2. This question has two parts. First, answer Part A. Then, answer Part B.

   Part A: What kind of figurative language is Douglass using when he writes, "This bread I used to **bestow** upon the hungry little urchins, who, in return, would give me that more valuable bread of knowledge"?

   ○ A. simile

   ○ B. metaphor

   ○ C. personification

   ○ D. verbal Irony

   Part B: What does the figurative language identified in Part A tell us about how Douglass feels about knowledge?

   ○ A. Douglass knows that the boys should value knowledge as much as he does, but they prefer bread.

   ○ B. Douglass knows that he needs to share knowledge, just like he shared bread with the boys from his neighborhood.

   ○ C. Douglass sees knowledge as a form of nourishment. Bread can nourish people who are hungry, and knowledge can nourish people who want to learn.

   ○ D. Douglass sees knowledge as something that can go stale if you do not use it, so he shares bread and knowledge with the boys in his neighborhood.

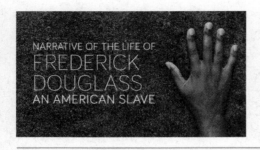

Close Read

Reread *Narrative of the Life of Frederick Douglass, An American Slave*. As you reread, complete the Skills Focus questions below. Then use your answers and annotations from the questions to help you complete the Write activity.

◎ SKILLS FOCUS

1. Autobiographical texts such as *Narrative of the Life of Frederick Douglass, An American Slave* utilize key details from the author's perspective. Identify a strong opinion that Douglass shares, and explain how it helps to reveal his purpose.

2. Identify details that reveal Douglass's central or main idea in this excerpt from *Narrative of the Life of Frederick Douglass, An American Slave*. Explain how the textual evidence supports that central or main idea.

3. Reread the final two paragraphs in the excerpt. Identify the informational elements within these two paragraphs. Use and cite at least two specific examples in your response.

4. Identify specific instances of figurative language Douglass uses to describe slavery and freedom, and explain what the language helps you understand about Douglass's message.

5. What chances did Frederick Douglass take? Why do you think he took them?

✏ WRITE

COMPARE AND CONTRAST: The speakers of the poems "Mother to Son" and "Learning to Read," and Frederick Douglass in his autobiography, describe the risks involved to make successes of their lives. While Douglass's autobiography uses informational text elements to convey his experience, all three texts send a message about the importance of education. Think about the use of language, descriptions, and events, and explain how they contribute to this message.

The Day I Saved a Life

INFORMATIONAL TEXT
Thomas Ponce
2018

Introduction

Thomas Ponce (b. 2000) is a Florida native, animal rights activist, and citizen lobbyist. He has been a vegetarian since age four, and at age five began writing about animal rights. He is the creator of the group Lobby for Animals, and he has received awards from major organizations such as PETA and the Farm Animal Rights Movement. In "The Day I Saved a Life," Ponce describes a key day in his life, which would lead directly to a greater awareness about the plight of sharks and his decision to actively work to improve their conditions.

"I swear the shark looked at me with gratitude. He was alive because I spoke up for him and he knew it."

NOTES

Skill: Technical Language

Fossilized is technical language. The context tells me fossilized teeth are really old. The dictionary definition of *fossilized* supports this: "to change into a fossil," which is "the remains or trace of an ancient life form." Now I know both *fossil* and *fossilized*.

Skill: Context Clues

I'm not sure what a scooper is, but it's a noun because *my* comes before it. He uses it to dig into the sand. I see *scoop* in *scooper*, and later he uses *scoop* to mean the same thing. It must be a tool used to scoop up sand.

1   We've all seen Hollywood's depiction of sharks, the media's over-dramatization of shark attacks and felt that pit in our stomach at the sight of a shark. Movies like *Jaws*, *Day of the Shark*, *Shark Night*, *Deep Blue Sea*, etc., give us the impression of a mindless killing machine out to kill all human beings. Well, I've seen another side of the shark and I've seen it up close and personal.

2   It all started on December 16, 2011, my birthday. My family took me to Venice Beach, which is also known as Shark Tooth Beach. This was the trip I had been waiting for. I had seen this location on the Discovery Channel over a year ago and had wanted to go ever since. Having the opportunity to find fossilized shark teeth that have been in the waters for over millions of years was something I was **ecstatic** about! When we arrived at our destination, I was amazed at all the sights, sounds and smells. The water was crystal clear and blue and the sand was so warm between my toes. The occasional breeze whisked my mind away to a beautiful tropical paradise. It was a perfect day to go sifting for shark teeth. I walked into the water up to my knees, sifter in hand, and began sifting. I dug my scooper into the sand, beneath the water, and pulled up many small teeth. I found great white teeth, bull shark teeth, tiger shark teeth and a few I was unsure about, it was amazing. Then it happened. I hit the jackpot! I discovered in my scoop the largest tooth I had ever seen. It was four inches long and black in color. Its edges were serrated and you could still see the gum line. The great white teeth I found paled in comparison to this massive tooth. It was a Megalodon tooth! My dream had come true, I had found one! This was the best birthday present I could have ever gotten, or so I thought.

3   As we were leaving the beach, a friendly local told us about a pier close by that was a perfect place to watch the sunset. I was determined to see the green flash that everyone talks about when the sun sets. We headed back to our hotel to change and then went straight to the pier. The view from the pier was miraculous. The skies were clear and the weather was perfect for being outside, not too hot and there was a cool breeze coming off the water. As we watched the sunset, the sky turned orange and pink as the sun went down. It was absolutely breathtaking! In the water we saw dolphins swimming and a man painting sea turtles at the edge of the pier. It was a night right out of a novel.

4   As we were leaving the pier I saw a fisherman pull a baby bonnethead shark up on his line. He pulled him onto the pier, hooting and hollering about his catch and how he was "going to eat tonight." The fisherman then started sharpening his very large knife, readying himself to gut the shark right then and there. The shark flapped and shook, grasping to hold onto life. It was horrible to see. I knew I had to do something,

One of a pair of new Bonnethead sharks at Chessington World of Adventures, Surrey, England

so I approached the fisherman and asked him to set the shark free. I explained how it was a living creature, a baby with a family and that it deserved to live. I explained to him the important role sharks play in our ecosystem. I pleaded with him to free him and not eat him. I even offered to buy him dinner. I told him how sharks are **keystone** species and how they keep the ocean ecosystem in balance; I explained about their slow reproductive rate and how we needed every shark in the ocean to keep it healthy. I explained how the effects of removing sharks would be felt throughout the ecosystem like a domino effect. I was not letting up, I knew I had to keep fighting for that shark. After what seemed like an eternity, the fisherman finally **conceded** and told me that I could set him free. I couldn't believe it, I did it! I immediately walked over, picked up the shark and placed him back into the water and told him to live free. I swear the shark looked at me with gratitude. He was alive because I spoke up for him and he knew it. I saw the understanding in his eyes and knew there was much more to sharks than what I had been led to believe.

5   That day changed me forever and now I fight for sharks' rights. I have always been an active animal and environmental advocate and a vegetarian and now vegan. I had run many fundraisers for farm animals and for spaying and neutering your pets. I had leafletted about animals in captivity and in **vivisection** labs; I had signed petitions against animal cruelty and protested at various sites where cruelty had been taking place, but until that day I hadn't really concentrated my efforts on sharks. I started doing some research and I watched a documentary called *Sharkwater* and it gave me insight into the plight of the shark. It showed me the horrors they faced due to finning. They were being killed in huge quantities for their fins and were becoming extremely close to extinction. The sharks are stripped of their fins then discarded, while still alive, back into the ocean. It was a horrible discovery and one that moved me to act and speak up for the sharks. From that moment on, I have dedicated myself to making as many people aware of what's going on with sharks as I can. My hope is that through educating people on the cruel and inhumane acts being done to sharks and by explaining the importance of sharks to the ocean ecosystem, as well as our own environment,

Please note that excerpts and passages in the StudySync® library and this workbook are intended as touchstones to generate interest in an author's work. The excerpts and passages do not substitute for the reading of entire texts, and StudySync® strongly recommends that students seek out and purchase the whole literary or informational work in order to experience it as the author intended. Links to online resellers are available in our digital library. In addition, complete works may be ordered through an authorized reseller by filling out and returning to StudySync® the order form enclosed in this workbook.

Reading & Writing Companion   **69**

that I can make a difference in helping to preserve this beautiful species. I hope to one day soon be speaking at Congress on behalf of sharks and **lobbying** to bring change to the finning laws in our country.

6   December 16, 2011 the ocean gave me two gifts, a Megalodon tooth and an appreciation and love of sharks. In return, I gave it back one of its own and a voice that could be heard and would never be silenced.

By Thomas Ponce, President and Founder of Lobby For Animals. Used by permission of Thomas Ponce.

First Read

Read "The Day I Saved a Life." After you read, complete the Think Questions below.

1. How does the author show his love of sharks? Provide specific examples from the text.

2. What effect does the author's sensory description of the beautiful evening at the pier have on the story? What is its function in the text? Use specific evidence from the text to support your answer.

3. What changed specifically for the author on this particular day? How was his life different afterward? Provide specific examples from the text.

4. Based on the context, what do you think the word **ecstatic** means? Write your definition here, and indicate which context clues informed your thinking.

5. Use context clues to determine the meaning of the word **concede** as it used in the text. Write your definition of *concede* here, and state which clues from the text helped you determine the answer. Confirm your definition using a print or online dictionary.

Please note that excerpts and passages in the StudySync® library and this workbook are intended as touchstones to generate interest in an author's work. The excerpts and passages do not substitute for the reading of entire texts, and StudySync® strongly recommends that students seek out and purchase the whole literary or informational work in order to experience it as the author intended. Links to online resellers are available in our digital library. In addition, complete works may be ordered through an authorized reseller by filling out and returning to StudySync® the order form enclosed in this workbook.

Reading & Writing Companion   **71**

Skill:
Context Clues

Use the Checklist to analyze Context Clues in "The Day I Saved a Life." Refer to the sample student annotations about Context Clues in the text.

••• CHECKLIST FOR CONTEXT CLUES

In order to use context as a clue to infer the meaning of a word or phrase, note the following:

- ✓ clues about the word's part of speech

- ✓ clues about the word's meaning in the surrounding text

- ✓ signal words that cue a type of context clue, such as:

  - *for example* or *for instance* to signal an example clue
  - *like, similarly,* or *just as* to signal a comparison clue
  - *but*, *however*, or *unlike* to signal a contrast clue

To determine the meaning of a word or phrase as it is used in a text, consider the following questions:

- ✓ What is the overall sentence, paragraph, or text about?

- ✓ How does the word function in the sentence?

- ✓ What clues can help me determine the word's part of speech?

- ✓ What text clues can help me figure out the word's definition?

- ✓ Are there any examples that show what the word means?

- ✓ What do I think the word means?

To verify the preliminary determination of the meaning of the word or phrase based on context, consider the following questions:

- ✓ Does the definition I inferred make sense within the context of the sentence?

- ✓ Which of the dictionary's definitions makes sense within the context of the sentence?

Skill:
Context Clues

Reread paragraph 4 of "The Day I Saved a Life." Then, using the Checklist on the previous page, answer the multiple-choice questions below.

⟳ YOUR TURN

1. What is the meaning of "domino effect"? Use context clues to figure out what the phrase means.

   ○ A. Killing is a serious thing and not to be taken lightly, like a game.
   ○ B. If one thing happens, it will cause another, and so on.
   ○ C. One good turn deserves another.
   ○ D. The world is a complex place, intricately structured.

2. Which quote from the text best supports the reasoning you used in question 1?

   ○ A. "The shark flapped and shook, grasping to hold onto life. It was horrible to see."
   ○ B. "I was not letting up, I knew I had to keep fighting for that shark."
   ○ C. "I explained to him the important role sharks play in our ecosystem. . . . I explained how the effects of removing sharks would be felt throughout the ecosystem."
   ○ D. "I swear the shark looked at me with gratitude. He was alive because I spoke up for him and he knew it."

3. What is the meaning of *conceded* as it used in the paragraph? Use context clues to figure out what the word means.

   ○ A. refused
   ○ B. argued
   ○ C. gave up
   ○ D. insisted

Please note that excerpts and passages in the StudySync® library and this workbook are intended as touchstones to generate interest in an author's work. The excerpts and passages do not substitute for the reading of entire texts, and StudySync® strongly recommends that students seek out and purchase the whole literary or informational work in order to experience it as the author intended. Links to online resellers are available in our digital library. In addition, complete works may be ordered through an authorized reseller by filling out and returning to StudySync® the order form enclosed in this workbook.

Reading & Writing Companion   **73**

Skill:
Technical Language

Use the Checklist to analyze Technical Language in "The Day I Saved a Life." Refer to the sample student annotations about Technical Language in the text.

••• CHECKLIST FOR TECHNICAL LANGUAGE

In order to determine the meaning of words and phrases as they are used in a text, note the following:

- ✓ the subject of the book or article

- ✓ any unfamiliar words that you think might be technical terms

- ✓ words that have multiple meanings that change when used with a specific subject

- ✓ the possible contextual meaning of a word, or the definition from a dictionary

To determine the meaning of words and phrases as they are used in a text, including technical meanings, consider the following questions:

- ✓ What is the subject of the informational text?

- ✓ How does the use of technical language help establish the author as an authority on the subject?

- ✓ Are there any technical words that have an impact on the meaning and tone, or quality, of the book or article?

- ✓ Does the writer use analogies, or a comparison between two things for the purpose of explanation or clarification? What impact do they have on your understanding of the subject?

- ✓ Does the writer use any allusions to another topic or subject as a way to explain something? What impact do they have on the author's treatment of the main subject?

Skill:
Technical Language

Reread paragraph 4 of "The Day I Saved a Life." Then, using the Checklist on the previous page, answer the multiple-choice questions below.

⟳ YOUR TURN

1. What is the meaning of the technical term *ecosystem*?

   ○ A. the world's oceans and the flow of water between them
   ○ B. the network of animals and plants that interact in an environment
   ○ C. a species of animal that lives in one place
   ○ D. planet Earth and all the living things on it

2. What is the meaning of the technical term *keystone species*?

   ○ A. an animal that eats both plants and animals
   ○ B. an animal that can survive in only one place
   ○ C. an animal that preys constantly and never stops hunting
   ○ D. an animal that plays a crucial role in its environment

3. Which quote from the text best supports the reasoning you used in question 2?

   ○ A. "The shark flapped and shook, grasping to hold onto life."
   ○ B. "I explained how it was a living creature, a baby with a family"
   ○ C. "I explained about their slow reproductive rate"
   ○ D. "I explained how the effects of removing sharks would be felt throughout the ecosystem"

Please note that excerpts and passages in the StudySync® library and this workbook are intended as touchstones to generate interest in an author's work. The excerpts and passages do not substitute for the reading of entire texts, and StudySync® strongly recommends that students seek out and purchase the whole literary or informational work in order to experience it as the author intended. Links to online resellers are available in our digital library. In addition, complete works may be ordered through an authorized reseller by filling out and returning to StudySync® the order form enclosed in this workbook.

Reading & Writing Companion 75

Close Read

Reread "The Day I Saved a Life." As you reread, complete the Skills Focus questions below. Then use your answers and annotations from the questions to help you complete the Write activity.

◎ SKILLS FOCUS

1. Explain the meaning of *finning* in paragraph 5, and discuss how and why this technical term helps make Ponce's argument more meaningful and gives it more of an impact.

2. Use context clues to determine the meaning of *jackpot*. How does this help to describe Ponce's discoveries? Does it make everything else he describes seem more important or less so? Use specific evidence from the text to support your answer.

3. Use context clues to determine the meaning of *extinction*. Is this word positive or negative? Is it contrasted with any other word in the text? How does it compare to the rest of the text that surrounds it? Use specific evidence from the text to support your response.

4. What is the meaning of the technical term *vegan*? Does it help Ponce's argument to use this term? Why or why not? Cite specific evidence from the text to support your answer.

5. What was risky about Thomas Ponce's actions? Would you have made the same decision that he did? Why or why not? What does Ponce seem to have learned from his experience?

✏ WRITE

ARGUMENTATIVE: Using Ponce's essay as a point of reference, write a persuasive essay where you defend a subject about which you are passionate. Be sure to include technical language where applicable, as this can lend authority to your opinions and ideas.

The Call of the Wild

FICTION
Jack London
1903

Introduction

Author Jack London (1876–1916) was a writer and adventurer, beginning his life in the San Francisco Bay area, and then traveling the world—seal hunting in the Far East, mucking for gold in the Yukon Territory, sailing the South Pacific, and more. While participating in the Klondike Gold Rush, he reportedly encountered a mythical wolf that served as the inspiration for *The Call of the Wild*, his most popular novel. The book details the adventures of Buck, a large and powerful St. Bernard mix, as he experiences both love and abuse from a succession of owners. In this excerpt, Buck, by now a sled dog, stirs up rebellion among the team when he stands up to the aggressive alpha dog, Spitz.

"He was ranging at the head of the pack, running the wild thing down"

NOTES

from Chapter III, The Dominant Primordial Beast

1 They made Sixty Mile, which is a fifty-mile run, on the first day; and the second day saw them booming up the Yukon well on their way to Pelly. But such splendid running was achieved not without great trouble and vexation on the part of Francois. The insidious revolt led by Buck had destroyed the **solidarity** of the team. It no longer was as one dog leaping in the

Dog sled in Alaska, circa 1890s

traces. The encouragement Buck gave the rebels led them into all kinds of petty misdemeanors. No more was Spitz a leader greatly to be feared. The old awe departed, and they grew equal to challenging his authority. Pike robbed him of half a fish one night, and gulped it down under the protection of Buck. Another night Dub and Joe fought Spitz and made him forego the punishment they deserved. And even Billee, the good-natured, was less good-natured, and whined not half so **placatingly** as in former days. Buck never came near Spitz without snarling and bristling menacingly. In fact, his conduct approached that of a bully, and he was given to swaggering up and down before Spitz's very nose.

2 The breaking down of discipline likewise affected the dogs in their relations with one another. They quarrelled and bickered more than ever among themselves, till at times the camp was a howling bedlam. Dave and Sol-leks alone were unaltered, though they were made irritable by the unending squabbling. Francois swore strange barbarous oaths, and stamped the snow in futile rage, and tore his hair. His lash was always singing among the dogs, but it was of small avail. Directly his back was turned they were at it again. He backed up Spitz with his whip, while Buck backed up the remainder of the team. Francois knew he was behind all the trouble, and Buck knew he knew; but Buck was too clever ever again to be caught red-handed. He worked faithfully in the harness, for the toil had become a delight to him; yet it was a

Skill:
Media

In both types of media, Buck's attitude about work changed. In the video, Buck wants to please his master, and so he happily changes his mind. The text is different. Buck seems to enjoy working but also enjoys causing trouble.

greater delight slyly to **precipitate** a fight amongst his mates and tangle the traces.

3   At the mouth of the Tahkeena, one night after supper, Dub turned up a snowshoe rabbit, blundered it, and missed. In a second the whole team was in full cry. A hundred yards away was a camp of the Northwest Police, with fifty dogs, huskies all, who joined the chase. The rabbit sped down the river, turned off into a small creek, up the frozen bed of which it held steadily. It ran lightly on the surface of the snow, while the dogs ploughed through by main strength. Buck led the pack, sixty strong, around bend after bend, but he could not gain. He lay down low to the race, whining eagerly, his splendid body flashing forward, leap by leap, in the wan white moonlight. And leap by leap, like some pale frost wraith, the snowshoe rabbit flashed on ahead.

4   All that stirring of old instincts which at stated periods drives men out from the sounding cities to forest and plain to kill things by chemically **propelled** leaden pellets, the blood lust, the joy to kill—all this was Buck's, only it was infinitely more intimate. He was ranging at the head of the pack, running the wild thing down, the living meat, to kill with his own teeth and wash his muzzle to the eyes in warm blood.

5   There is an ecstasy that marks the summit of life, and beyond which life cannot rise. And such is the **paradox** of living, this ecstasy comes when one is most alive, and it comes as a complete forgetfulness that one is alive. This ecstasy, this forgetfulness of living, comes to the artist, caught up and out of himself in a sheet of flame; it comes to the soldier, war-mad on a stricken field and refusing quarter; and it came to Buck, leading the pack, sounding the old wolf-cry, straining after the food that was alive and that fled swiftly before him through the moonlight. He was sounding the deeps of his nature, and of the parts of his nature that were deeper than he, going back into the womb of Time. He was mastered by the sheer surging of life, the tidal wave of being, the perfect joy of each separate muscle, joint, and sinew in that it was everything that was not death, that it was aglow and rampant, expressing itself in movement, flying exultantly under the stars and over the face of dead matter that did not move.

London, Jack. *The Call of the Wild*. 1903. Scholastic Paperbacks, 2001.

Skill:
Language, Style,
and Audience

The author compares the speed of Buck and the rabbit using "leap by leap" and the word "flashed." Buck's chase of the rabbit comes alive through this analogy. It is written in an active way and draws me into the story.

First Read

Read *The Call of the Wild*. After you read, complete the Think Questions below.

☁ THINK QUESTIONS

1. Refer to several details in paragraph 1 to explain how Buck "destroyed the solidarity of the team." Cite evidence that is directly stated in the text, and make inferences to support your explanation.

2. What evidence is there in paragraph 2 that Buck took pleasure in causing trouble for Francois?

3. How did Buck react when Dub turned up a snowshoe rabbit? What inferences can you make about Buck from his behavior? Support your answer with specific evidence from the text.

4. Use context to determine the meaning of the word **paradox** as it is used in paragraph 5. Write your definition of *paradox* and tell how you determined the meaning of the word. Then check your definition in a print or digital dictionary to confirm the word's meaning.

5. By understanding that the Latin word *placare* means "to calm down" or "appease," use the context clues provided in paragraph 1 to determine the meaning of **placatingly**. Write your definition of *placatingly* and tell how you determined the meaning of the word.

Skill:
Language, Style, and Audience

Use the Checklist to analyze Language, Style, and Audience in *The Call of the Wild*. Refer to the sample student annotations about Language, Style, and Audience in the text.

••• CHECKLIST FOR LANGUAGE, STYLE, AND AUDIENCE

In order to determine an author's style, do the following:

- ✓ identify and define any unfamiliar words or phrases

- ✓ use context, including the meaning of surrounding words and phrases

- ✓ note possible reactions to the author's word choice

- ✓ examine your reaction to the author's word choice

- ✓ identify any analogies, or comparisons in which one part of the comparison helps explain the other

To analyze the impact of specific word choice on meaning and tone, ask the following questions:

- ✓ How did your understanding of the language change during your analysis?

- ✓ How does the writer's word choice impact or create meaning in the text?

- ✓ How does the writer's word choice impact or create a specific tone in the text?

- ✓ How could various audiences interpret this language? What different possible emotional responses can you list?

- ✓ What analogies do I see here? Where might an analogy have clarified meaning or created a specific tone?

Skill:
Language, Style, and Audience

Reread paragraph 5 of *The Call of the Wild*. Then, using the Checklist on the previous page, answer the multiple-choice questions below.

↻ YOUR TURN

1. By using the phrase "There is an ecstasy that marks the summit of life, and beyond which life cannot rise," what is Jack London trying to say about Buck?

   ○ A. That Buck is not fast enough to catch and kill the rabbit.
   ○ B. That Buck is about to kill the rabbit.
   ○ C. That Buck could not possibly feel more alive than he is right now.
   ○ D. That Buck is about to die.

2. Why does Jack London mention life and death throughout his analogies about Buck and the rabbit?

   ○ A. He wants to suggest that Buck will die once he kills the rabbit.
   ○ B. He is trying to say that Buck is dying.
   ○ C. He wants to draw a comparison between life and death and the act of Buck chasing the rabbit.
   ○ D. He is trying to make everyone who reads the story feel bad for the rabbit.

3. What is the meaning behind the author's phrase "it comes to the soldier, war-mad and refusing quarter"?

   ○ A. That a soldier driven crazy by battle will still fight on and refuse the safety of shelter.
   ○ B. That a soldier driven crazy by battle will not be paid.
   ○ C. That a soldier driven crazy by battle will refuse to get paid.
   ○ D. That soldiers always refuse safety in order to get paid.

Skill:
Media

Use the Checklist to analyze Media in *The Call of the Wild*. Refer to the sample student annotations about Media in the text.

••• CHECKLIST FOR MEDIA

In order to determine the extent to which a filmed or live production of a story or drama stays faithful to or departs from the text or script, do the following:

- ✓ note key elements from the text and how they changed or were removed in the film

- ✓ think about the advantages and disadvantages of using different media to present a particular topic, idea, or event

- ✓ consider the choices made by the director of a film, and how they may emphasize or minimize an event or even a line of dialogue from a written work

- ✓ weigh and understand the strengths and weaknesses of different media

To analyze the extent to which a filmed or live production of a story or drama stays faithful to or departs from the text or script, and to evaluate the choices made by the director or actors, ask the following questions:

- ✓ How does the filmed production of a story stay faithful to or depart from the text?

- ✓ What are the strengths of different media, such as novels or motion pictures, when telling a story? What are their weaknesses?

- ✓ How might the choices a director makes when making a film based on a novel completely change the point of view?

Please note that excerpts and passages in the StudySync® library and this workbook are intended as touchstones to generate interest in an author's work. The excerpts and passages do not substitute for the reading of entire texts, and StudySync® strongly recommends that students seek out and purchase the whole literary or informational work in order to experience it as the author intended. Links to online resellers are available in our digital library. In addition, complete works may be ordered through an authorized reseller by filling out and returning to StudySync® the order form enclosed in this workbook.

Reading & Writing Companion   **83**

Skill:
Media

Reread paragraph 4 of *The Call of the Wild*, and rewatch the video clip of *The Call of the Wild* from 03:57 to 05:20, available on the StudySync site. Then, using the Checklist on the previous page, answer the multiple-choice questions below.

↻ YOUR TURN

1. What is Buck's reason for pursuing food in the text?

   O A. Francois didn't give him any food, and he was hungry.
   O B. He pulled 1,000 pounds, and that made him really hungry.
   O C. He was going to eat the snowshoe rabbit, but Dub stole it from him.
   O D. His instincts——in particular, the joy to kill——are what give him the desire to pursue food.

2. In the video, why does Buck finally eat so hungrily?

   O A. He seems to trust and understand that John Thornton is there to help him and wants him to be happy.
   O B. He pulled 1,000 pounds, and that made him really hungry.
   O C. He has to sneak food from John Thornton, so he eats it as quickly as he can.
   O D. His instincts as a dog make him eat quickly.

3. What is the difference in the portrayal of these scenes in the text and in the video clip?

   O A. In the text, the food is rabbit, but in the video, the food is moose.
   O B. Buck has different reasons for seeking food. Also, he relies on Francois in the text, but he relies only on himself in the video.
   O C. Buck has different reasons for seeking food. Also, he relies on Thornton in the video, but he relies only on himself in the text.
   O D. Buck moves slowly in the text and quickly in the video.

Close Read

Reread *The Call of the Wild* and rewatch the video clip of *The Call of the Wild* available on the StudySync site. As you reread, complete the Skills Focus questions below. Then use your answers and annotations from the questions to help you complete the Write activity.

◎ SKILLS FOCUS

1. Reread paragraph 2. What message is the author trying to convey about control? Include important details from the text that support your answer.

2. Reread paragraph 5 and identify an analogy. Explain what the analogy means and why you think it was important for Jack London to phrase his text that way.

3. Identify a part in the excerpt where humans interact with Buck and the dogs. Explain their interaction(s), and contrast this scene with what you saw in the video. How is this scene treated differently between the two types of media?

4. Based on your observations of the video and having read the text, who was taking a bigger chance: Buck, Thornton, the pack, or Francois? Make specific references from both the video and the text to support your response.

✎ WRITE

LITERARY ANALYSIS: In the final paragraph, Jack London writes, "such is the paradox of living, this ecstasy comes when one is most alive, and it comes as a complete forgetfulness that one is alive." Based on his language, what sort of response was he likely looking for from his audience? Is there a difference in the impact of the text and the impact of the video? Which medium is more powerful and effective? Use textual evidence as well as references from the video to support your response.

Please note that excerpts and passages in the StudySync® library and this workbook are intended as touchstones to generate interest in an author's work. The excerpts and passages do not substitute for the reading of entire texts, and StudySync® strongly recommends that students seek out and purchase the whole literary or informational work in order to experience it as the author intended. Links to online resellers are available in our digital library. In addition, complete works may be ordered through an authorized reseller by filling out and returning to StudySync® the order form enclosed in this workbook.

Reading & Writing Companion   **85**

Cocoon

POETRY
Mahvash Sabet
2013

Introduction

————————————————————————————

Mahvash Sabet (b. 1953), a leader in the Bahá'í community in Tehran, Iran, was arrested and imprisoned at Evin Prison in March of 2008 because of her faith. The Iranian government does not recognize the Bahá'í Faith as an official religion, even though it is the largest religious minority in the country. Before her arrest, Sabet worked as a teacher, collaborating with the National Literacy Committee and serving as director of the Bahá'í Institute for Higher Education for 15 years. While in prison, Sabet began writing poems, which were smuggled out by relatives and were eventually translated into English by Bahiyyih Nakhjavani. *Prison Poems*, a collection of about 70 of Sabet's poems, was published in 2013. After nearly ten years of imprisonment, Sabet was released in September of 2017. "Cocoon" depicts a speaker wrestling with contradictory feelings.

"I'm tossed to and fro, from here to there . . ."

1   There's a part of me that keeps mourning
2   for the soft cocoon where I lay,
3   a part of me that keeps pining
4   for the delicate **chrysalis** smashed and destroyed
5   before my eyes that day.

6   I'm tossed to and fro, from here to there,
7   caught between **compulsions**;
8   I'm thrown left and right and back and forth,
9   longing for the freedom of flight and yet
10 **craving** those soft consolations.

11 When my soul broke free, a part of me
12 **thrilled** at the lift of its arc,
13 but another shrank back in cowering fear
14 from the threatening fires, from the lowering smoke
15 that awaited me in here.

16 All this makes me wonder greatly
17 about **contrary** desires.
18 There's something in me approves of flying,
19 applauds the thought of bravely dying,
20 yet I weep for the cocoon's demise.

From *Prison Poems*, 2013. Used by permission of George Ronald Publishing Ltd.

NOTES

Skill:
Connotation and Denotation

The denotative meaning of cocoon *is a case that insect larva spin as protection when turning into an adult. The connotative meaning here seems to be a bed, a safe place that the speaker remembers before she was arrested and imprisoned.*

Please note that excerpts and passages in the StudySync® library and this workbook are intended as touchstones to generate interest in an author's work. The excerpts and passages do not substitute for the reading of entire texts, and StudySync® strongly recommends that students seek out and purchase the whole literary or informational work in order to experience it as the author intended. Links to online resellers are available in our digital library. In addition, complete works may be ordered through an authorized reseller by filling out and returning to StudySync® the order form enclosed in this workbook.

Reading & Writing Companion   87

First Read

Read "Cocoon." After you read, complete the Think Questions below.

 THINK QUESTIONS

1. In lines 1–5, what is the speaker mourning? Cite evidence from the text to support your answer.

2. What do lines 6–10 tell you about the speaker's state of mind? Support your answer with evidence from the text.

3. The speaker says in lines 11–15 that a part of her felt thrilled "when my soul broke free." What other emotion does she describe? Cite evidence from the text to support your answer.

4. What is the meaning of the word **craving** as it is used in the text? Write your best definition here, along with a brief explanation of how you arrived at its meaning, and then consult a dictionary to check your answer.

5. The Latin word *contra* means "against." With this information in mind and using context clues from the text, write your best definition of the word **contrary** here.

Skill:
Connotation and Denotation

Use the Checklist to analyze Connotation and Denotation in "Cocoon." Refer to the sample student annotations about Connotation and Denotation in the text.

••• CHECKLIST FOR CONNOTATION AND DENOTATION

In order to identify the denotative meanings of words, use the following steps:

✓ first, note unfamiliar words and phrases, keywords used to describe important characters, events, and ideas, or words that inspire or cause an emotional reaction

✓ next, determine and note the denotative meaning of a word by checking a reference source, such as a dictionary, glossary, or thesaurus

To better understand the meanings of words and phrases as they are used in a text, including connotative meanings, use the following questions:

✓ How do synonyms or context help you identify the connotative meaning of the word?

✓ How could you say this word or phrase differently? Would it change or maintain the meaning of the sentence/line/paragraph?

✓ How can you note differences between words with similar denotations and their connotations?

To determine the meaning of words and phrases as they are used in a text, including connotative meanings, use the following questions:

✓ What is the meaning of the word or phrase? What is its denotation, and what connotations does the word or phrase have?

✓ If I substitute a synonym based on denotation, is the meaning the same? How does it change the meaning of the text?

Please note that excerpts and passages in the StudySync® library and this workbook are intended as touchstones to generate interest in an author's work. The excerpts and passages do not substitute for the reading of entire texts, and StudySync® strongly recommends that students seek out and purchase the whole literary or informational work in order to experience it as the author intended. Links to online resellers are available in our digital library. In addition, complete works may be ordered through an authorized reseller by filling out and returning to StudySync® the order form enclosed in this workbook.

Reading & Writing Companion   89

Skill:
Connotation and Denotation

Reread lines 11–20 of "Cocoon." Then, using the Checklist on the previous page, answer the multiple-choice questions below.

♻ YOUR TURN

1. In lines 11 and 12, the speaker writes, "When my soul broke free, a part of me / thrilled at the lift of its arc." What word could you use in place of *thrilled* that would have the same connotation and maintain, or keep, the meaning of the line?

   ○ A. When my soul broke free, a part of me / was happy at the lift of its arc

   ○ B. When my soul broke free, a part of me / was surprised at the lift of its arc.

   ○ C. When my soul broke free, a part of me / was exhilarated at the lift of its arc.

   ○ D. When my soul broke free, a part of me / was pleased at the lift of its arc.

2. *Shrank* is the past tense of *shrink*, which means "to become smaller because of cold, heat, or moisture." Does the way the speaker uses the word *shrank* in line 13 have a negative or a positive connotation?

   ○ A. Since only part of the author shrank back in cowering fear, the use of the word has a neutral connotation, neither positive nor negative.

   ○ B. The speaker shrinks because of heat from a threatening fire, so *shrank* has a negative connotation.

   ○ C. The speaker is thrilled because her soul has broken free, so the use of *shrank* in the third line has a positive connotation.

   ○ D. The speaker shrinks because of fear, not because of heat, cold, or moisture, so she uses its negative connotation.

COCOON

Close Read

Reread "Cocoon." As you reread, complete the Skills Focus questions below. Then use your answers and annotations from the questions to help you complete the Write activity.

◎ SKILLS FOCUS

1. The words *smashed* and *destroyed* in the first stanza (lines 1–5) have similar denotations. Which word has a stronger connotation, and why?

2. Reread lines 1–10. Identify words the author uses that have specific emotional connotations. Explain why you think the author chose these specific words.

3. Reread lines 11 and 12 in the third stanza. Does the word *broke* have a positive or a negative connotation the way it is used here? How could it be used so that it has a different connotation?

4. Why does the speaker consider the idea of freedom as taking a chance?

✏ WRITE

LITERARY ANALYSIS: In this poem, Mahvash Sabet describes the conflicting emotions she feels when she is arrested in her home and watches as it is destroyed. She then reflects on why she should feel torn between desiring freedom and wanting the security she once had. Some of the words she chooses to describe her feelings have powerful connotations that help her describe her experience. Write an analysis in which you explain Sabet's purpose for telling this story about her personal experience. Use textual evidence to support your response, including the author's use of connotation and denotation.

Please note that excerpts and passages in the StudySync® library and this workbook are intended as touchstones to generate interest in an author's work. The excerpts and passages do not substitute for the reading of entire texts, and StudySync® strongly recommends that students seek out and purchase the whole literary or informational work in order to experience it as the author intended. Links to online resellers are available in our digital library. In addition, complete works may be ordered through an authorized reseller by filling out and returning to StudySync® the order form enclosed in this workbook.

Reading & Writing Companion   91

Extended Writing Project and Grammar

EXTENDED WRITING PROJECT

INFORMATIVE WRITING

Informative Writing Process: Plan

| PLAN | DRAFT | REVISE | EDIT AND PUBLISH |

In a variety of genres, the authors of the texts in this unit explore the value of taking risks to achieve rewards. Whether one is learning to read, overcoming a terrible tragedy, or simply getting on with life, any decision can involve a risk. While there is always a chance that something will go wrong, often great, unforeseen opportunities come from risk-taking.

WRITING PROMPT

What happens when we take risks?

Choose three informational texts from this unit, including research links in the Blasts, and explain how the authors inform readers about their risk-taking subjects. Identify the risks individuals take and the outcomes of those risks. Include a clear main idea or thesis statement, and cite evidence from each text to explain your conclusions. Regardless of which sources you choose, be sure your essay includes the following:

- an introduction
- a main idea or thesis statement
- a clear text structure
- supporting details
- a conclusion

Writing to Sources

As you gather ideas and information from the texts in the unit, be sure to:

- use evidence from multiple sources; and
- avoid overly relying on one source.

Please note that excerpts and passages in the StudySync® library and this workbook are intended as touchstones to generate interest in an author's work. The excerpts and passages do not substitute for the reading of entire texts, and StudySync® strongly recommends that students seek out and purchase the whole literary or informational work in order to experience it as the author intended. Links to online resellers are available in our digital library. In addition, complete works may be ordered through an authorized reseller by filling out and returning to StudySync® the order form enclosed in this workbook.

Reading & Writing Companion   **93**

Introduction to Informative Writing

Informative writing informs readers about real people, places, things, and events. It includes ideas, concepts, and information that needs to be organized in a logical way such as definition, classification, compare/contrast, and cause/effect. Good informative writing also includes a clear thesis statement or main idea of the essay, and the writer develops that main idea with supporting details, such as descriptions, examples, reasons, quotations, and relevant facts. The characteristics of informative writing include:

- an introduction with a thesis statement or main idea
- supporting details that develop the thesis statement or main idea
- a clear and logical text structure
- a formal style
- a conclusion that wraps up your ideas

As you continue with this Extended Writing Project, you'll receive more instruction and practice at crafting each of the characteristics of informative writing to create your own informative essay.

Before you get started on your own informative essay, read this essay that one student, Aiko, wrote in response to the writing prompt. As you read the Model, highlight and annotate the features of informative writing that Aiko included in her essay.

Risks Teach Valuable Lessons

1 People take risks every day. Many risks are small, such as trying a new type of food. Other risks are bigger, such as moving across the country. Whether big or small, all risks have something in common. People can never be certain of how a risk will turn out. Every time a person takes a risk, there is a chance that they will lose something valuable. Frederick Douglass, the crew of the *Challenger*, and members of the Biloxi-Chitimacha-Choctaw Native American tribe are examples of people who have risked devastating losses to pursue worthy goals. Even though these risks and the outcomes of these risks differ, they all teach essential lessons.

2 In his autobiography *Narrative of the Life of Frederick Douglass, An American Slave*, Douglass describes dangerous risks that he took on the road to freedom. Born into slavery, Douglass was legally denied an education. When he was young, however, the mistress of one house started to teach him how to read until her husband told her to stop. She then became angry and violent when Douglass tried to learn on his own. Douglas recalls the rage: "I have had her rush at me with a face made all up of fury, and snatch from me a newspaper, in a manner that fully revealed her apprehension." Douglass knew that there could be serious personal and legal consequences if he were caught, but he decided that knowledge was worth the risk. Douglass saw knowledge as part of his long-term plan to escape slavery. He explains, "I looked forward to a time at which it would be safe for me to escape. I was too young to think of doing so immediately; besides, I wished to learn how to write, as I might have occasion to write my own pass." Douglass's efforts gave him a way to pursue freedom. After several years, he learned how to read and write. The risks Douglass took in pursuit of his goal also teach readers valuable lessons. His success teaches the values of perseverance and faith in one's own abilities.

NOTES

3   However, failure teaches lessons, too. In 1986, the crew of the space shuttle *Challenger* set out to make new discoveries in space, but they lost their lives in a space shuttle disaster. In his speech "Address to the Nation on the Explosion of the Space Shuttle *Challenger*," President Ronald Reagan reminds Americans that the crew was willing to do a dangerous job. They wanted to travel into space because they believed that the mission would be worth the risk. He says, "They had a hunger to explore the universe and discover its truths." The *Challenger* crew was well prepared and planning to study important questions about the universe. Unfortunately, they never had a chance to achieve that goal because the space shuttle exploded after takeoff. Despite this tragic end, Americans can still learn a valuable lesson from the *Challenger* crew. Reagan explains that "the future doesn't belong to the fainthearted; it belongs to the brave. The *Challenger* crew was pulling us into the future, and we'll continue to follow them." The crew was willing to risk their lives in search of knowledge about the universe. Their efforts teach the values of selflessness and bravery.

4   The risks that one needs to take to pursue a goal can also change over time. This is evident in "The Vanishing Island," an informational article by Anya Groner. In the early 1800s, many members of the Biloxi-Chitimacha-Choctaw Native American tribe established a community on a small island off the coast of Louisiana, and it became a "cultural homeland." The island is called Isle de Jean Charles. Since the mid-twentieth century, however, the land on the island has been rapidly eroding, or wearing away. Storms, river engineering, and pollution are causing this to happen, and the landform may not even exist by 2050. As a result, many members of the tribe will risk giving up their land and homes to relocate the community. Chief Naquin, the current chief of the Biloxi-Chitimacha-Choctaw Native American tribe, compared the loss of this island to "the loss of a family member." Leaving that land will be painful, but members are dedicated to preserving their history, community, and culture on the new site. For example, tribal secretary Chantel Comardelle envisions a museum that guides visitors through the history of the island. Many members of the community also value family. To encourage interactions among family members on the new site, they want to build groups of houses with shared backyards. These plans address important issues, but many residents on Isle de Jean Charles will

NOTES

still need to endure a difficult move. Their sacrifices teach readers the values of determination and resilience, the ability to recover from a loss.

5   *Narrative of the Life of Frederick Douglass, An American Slave,* "Address to the Nation on the Explosion of the Space Shuttle *Challenger*," and "The Vanishing Island" inform readers about historic risks that people have taken to pursue their goals. They show that each person faced hardships as a result of their decisions, and the *Challenger* crew tragically lost their lives. However, their stories continue to teach lessons about honorable qualities. They set examples that readers can follow when they need to decide if they want to take a risk for an important goal.

Please note that excerpts and passages in the StudySync® library and this workbook are intended as touchstones to generate interest in an author's work. The excerpts and passages do not substitute for the reading of entire texts, and StudySync® strongly recommends that students seek out and purchase the whole literary or informational work in order to experience it as the author intended. Links to online resellers are available in our digital library. In addition, complete works may be ordered through an authorized reseller by filling out and returning to StudySync® the order form enclosed in this workbook.

Reading & Writing Companion   97

✎ WRITE

Writers often take notes about their ideas before they sit down to write. Think about what you've learned so far about informative writing to help you begin prewriting.

- What are your ideas about what happens when people take risks? Is risk-taking positive or negative behavior? Why?

- Which three informational texts in the unit best reflect your ideas? Why?

- What risks do the people in those texts take?

- What do the outcomes of their risks tell you about risk-taking?

- How do the authors of those texts express their ideas about risk-taking?

- What textual evidence might you use to support your ideas?

Response Instructions

Use the questions in the bulleted list to write a one-paragraph summary. Your summary should describe the ideas that you want to share and how the texts support them.

Don't worry about including all of the details now; focus only on the most essential and important elements. You will refer back to this short summary as you continue through the steps of the writing process.

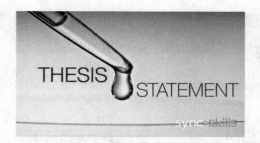

Skill:
Thesis Statement

••• CHECKLIST FOR THESIS STATEMENT

Before you begin writing your thesis statement, ask yourself the following questions:

- What is the prompt asking me to write about?

- What is the topic of my essay? How can I state it clearly for the reader?

- What claim do I want to make about the topic of this essay? Is my statement clear to my reader?

- Does my thesis statement introduce the body of my essay?

- Where should I place my thesis statement?

Here are some methods to introduce and develop your claim and topic clearly:

- Think about the topic and central idea of your essay.

  > The central idea of an argument is stated as a claim, or what will be proven or shown to be true.

  > Identify as many claims as you intend to prove.

- Write a clear statement about the central idea or claim. Your thesis statement should:

  > let the reader anticipate the body of your essay

  > respond completely to the writing prompt

- Consider the best placement for your thesis statement.

  > If your response is short, you may want to get right to the point. Your thesis statement may be presented in the first sentence of the essay.

  > If your response is longer (as in a formal essay), you can build up your thesis statement. In this case, you can place your thesis statement at the end of your introductory paragraph.

⟳ YOUR TURN

Read the phrases below. Then, complete the chart by sorting them into those that are thesis statements and those that are supporting details.

	Phrases
A	I lived in Master Hugh's family about seven years. During this time, I succeeded in learning to read and write. —From *Narrative of the Life of Frederick Douglass, An American Slave*
B	I immediately walked over, picked up the shark and placed him back into the water and told him to live free. I swear the shark looked at me with gratitude. He was alive because I spoke up for him and he knew it. —From "The Day I Saved a Life"
C	Today is a day for mourning and remembering. —From "Address to the Nation on the Explosion of the Space Shuttle *Challenger*"
D	If I was in a separate room any considerable length of time, I was sure to be suspected of having a book, and was at once called to give an account of myself. —From *Narrative of the Life of Frederick Douglass, An American Slave*
E	And perhaps we've forgotten the courage it took for the crew of the shuttle. But they, the *Challenger* Seven, were aware of the dangers, but overcame them and did their jobs brilliantly. —From "Address to the Nation on the Explosion of the Space Shuttle *Challenger*"
F	Movies like *Jaws, Day of the Shark, Shark Night, Deep Blue Sea,* etc., give us the impression of a mindless killing machine out to kill all human beings. Well, I've seen another side of the shark and I've seen it up close and personal. —From "The Day I Saved a Life"

Thesis Statement	Supporting Details

✏ WRITE

Use the questions in the checklist to revise the beginning of your informative essay.

Please note that excerpts and passages in the StudySync® library and this workbook are intended as touchstones to generate interest in an author's work. The excerpts and passages do not substitute for the reading of entire texts, and StudySync® strongly recommends that students seek out and purchase the whole literary or informational work in order to experience it as the author intended. Links to online resellers are available in our digital library. In addition, complete works may be ordered through an authorized reseller by filling out and returning to StudySync® the order form enclosed in this workbook.

Reading & Writing Companion   101

Skill:
Organizing Informative Writing

••• CHECKLIST FOR ORGANIZING INFORMATIVE WRITING

As you consider how to organize your writing for your informative essay, use the following questions as a guide:

• What is my topic? How can I summarize the main idea?

• How can I organize the information from the text into broad categories?

• What is the logical order of my ideas, concepts, and information? Do I see a pattern that is similar to a specific text structure?

• Which organizational structure should I use to present my information?

• How might using graphics, headings, or some form of multimedia help to present my information?

Here are some broader categories that can help you organize ideas, concepts, and information and aid comprehension:

• topic or main idea

• definitions, including restatements and examples

• classifications, including subcategories of a topic

• comparisons of ideas or concepts

• cause-and-effect relationships

⟳ YOUR TURN

Read the informational text titles below. Then, complete the chart by writing the organizational structure that would best convey the ideas of each text.

Organizational Structure Options			
compare/contrast	definition	classification	cause and effect

Informational Text Title	Organizational Structure
"What Is Ornithology?"	
"On Puffins and Penguins: An Exclusive Look at Their Similarities and Differences"	
"Why Can't Ostriches Fly?"	
"A Guide to Flightless Birds"	

⟳ YOUR TURN

Complete the chart below by writing a short summary of what you will focus on in each paragraph of your essay.

Outline	Summary
Introduction:	
Body Paragraph 1:	
Body Paragraph 2:	
Body Paragraph 3:	
Conclusion:	

Copyright © BookheadEd Learning, LLC

SUPPORTING DETAILS

sync●skills

Skill:
Supporting Details

As you look for supporting details to develop your topic, claim, or thesis statement, ask yourself the following questions:

- What is my main idea about this topic?
- What does a reader need to know about the topic in order to understand the main idea?
- What details will support my thesis statement?
- Is this information necessary to the reader's understanding of the topic?
- Does this information help to develop and refine my key concept or idea?
- Does this information relate closely to my thesis statement or claim?
- Where can I find better evidence that will provide stronger support for my point?

Here are some suggestions for how you can develop your topic:

- Review your thesis statement or claim.
- Consider your main idea.
- Note what the reader will need to know in order to understand the topic.
- Be sure to consult credible sources.
- Use different types of supporting details, such as:
  > well-chosen facts that are specific to your topic and enhance your discussion to establish credibility with your reader and build information

  > definitions to explain difficult concepts, terms, or ideas in your topic, claim, or thesis statement

  > concrete details that will add descriptive and detailed material to your topic

  > quotations to directly connect your thesis statement or claim to the text

  > examples and other information to deepen your claim, topic, or thesis statement

YOUR TURN

Choose the best answer to each question.

1. Aiko wants to improve the supporting details of a previous draft of her informative essay. How can she rewrite the underlined sentence to provide more support?

> In his autobiography *Narrative of the Life of Frederick Douglass, An American Slave*, Douglass describes many risks he took. However, Douglass is not the only person who took risks. <u>Some kids helped him.</u> This shows that it was also risky to agree to teach an enslaved person at the time.

- ○ A. Douglass knew some white children, and he says, "As many of these as I could, I converted into teachers."
- ○ B. Douglass gave bread to some boys, "who, in return, would give me that more valuable bread of knowledge."
- ○ C. Even though it was "almost an unpardonable offence to teach slaves to read in this Christian country," some local boys agreed to teach him.
- ○ D. Douglass recalls chatting with some white boys about slavery: "These words used to trouble them; they would express for me the liveliest sympathy."

2. Aiko would like to add a supporting detail to a previous draft of her paragraph on "Address to the Nation on the Explosion of the Space Shuttle *Challenger*." Which quotation could best follow and provide support for her last sentence?

> Failure can have a great impact on people, too. For example, when the crew of the *Challenger* died on their mission, the American people were deeply affected by the loss. The tragedy was a reminder that failure is part of success.

- ○ A. "Nineteen years ago, almost to the day, we lost three astronauts in a terrible accident on the ground. But we've never lost an astronaut in flight; we've never had a tragedy like this. And perhaps we've forgotten the courage it took for the crew of the shuttle."
- ○ B. "I know it is hard to understand, but sometimes painful things like this happen. It's all part of the process of exploration and discovery. It's all part of taking a chance and expanding man's horizons."
- ○ C. "I've always had great faith in and respect for our space program, and what happened today does nothing to diminish it. We don't hide our space program."
- ○ D. "We'll continue our quest in space. There will be more shuttle flights and more shuttle crews and, yes, more volunteers, more civilians, more teachers in space. Nothing ends here; our hopes and our journeys continue."

YOUR TURN

Complete the chart below by identifying evidence from each text you've chosen. Identifying evidence will help you develop your own thesis statement.

Text	Evidence
Selection #1:	
Selection #2:	
Selection #3:	

Informative Writing Process: Draft

PLAN	DRAFT	REVISE	EDIT AND PUBLISH

You have already made progress toward writing your informative essay. Now it is time to draft your informative essay.

 **WRITE**

Use your plan and other responses in your Binder to draft your informative essay. You may also have new ideas as you begin drafting. Feel free to explore those new ideas as you have them. You can also ask yourself these questions:

- Does my thesis statement or main idea of the essay clearly respond to the prompt?

- Does the organization of my essay make sense?

- Have I developed my thesis statement by using supporting details that help explain key ideas and are closely related to my topic?

- Have I made my ideas clear to readers?

Before you submit your draft, read it over carefully. You want to be sure that you've responded to all aspects of the prompt.

Please note that excerpts and passages in the StudySync® library and this workbook are intended as touchstones to generate interest in an author's work. The excerpts and passages do not substitute for the reading of entire texts, and StudySync® strongly recommends that students seek out and purchase the whole literary or informational work in order to experience it as the author intended. Links to online resellers are available in our digital library. In addition, complete works may be ordered through an authorized reseller by filling out and returning to StudySync® the order form enclosed in this workbook.

Reading & Writing Companion   **107**

Here is Aiko's informative essay draft. As you read, identify Aiko's main ideas. As she continues to revise and edit her essay, she will find and improve weak spots in her writing, as well as correct any language or punctuation mistakes.

NOTES

STUDENT MODEL: FIRST DRAFT

Risks Teach Valuable Lessons

~~Everybody takes risks even through they can never be certain of how a risk will turn out. Some risks are small. Some are big. Every time a person takes a risk, risking losing something. Frederick Douglass, the crew of the Challenger, and members of the Biloxi-Chitimacha-Choctaw Native American tribe all risked losses in to pursue their goals. The risks that they took were very different, but they all show that risk-taking can help people learn lessons.~~

People take risks every day. Many risks are small, such as trying a new type of food. Other risks are bigger, such as moving across the country. Whether big or small, all risks have something in common. People can never be certain of how a risk will turn out. Every time a person takes a risk, there is a chance that they will lose something valuable. Frederick Douglass, the crew of the *Challenger*, and members of the Biloxi-Chitimacha-Choctaw Native American tribe are examples of people who have risked devastating losses to pursue worthy goals. Even though these risks and the outcomes of these risks differ, they all teach essential lessons.

In his autobiography *Narrative of the Life of Frederick Douglass, An American Slave*, Douglass describes many dangerous risks taking. Born into slavery, Douglass was legaly denied an education. When he was young, the mistress of one house started to teach him how to read until her husband telling her to stop. She then got angry and violent when Douglass tried to learn on his own. Douglass says, "I have had her rush at me with a face made all up of fury, and snatch from me a newspaper, in a manner that fully revealed her apprehension." Still, Douglass, wanting to learn, he explains, "All this, however, was too late. The first step had been taken. Mistress, in teaching me the alphabet, had given me the *inch*, and no precaution could prevent me from taking the *ell*." Douglass's efforts made a difference. After several years, he learned how to read and writing.

Skill:
Introductions

Aiko adds more information about the people she will write about to clarify why she chose to analyze their stories in her essay. After reviewing these changes, Aiko sees that she still needs to engage readers at the beginning of her paragraph, so she adds a new sentence as a hook. After making those changes, Aiko then revises her thesis statement so that it flows from her new ideas.

The risks Douglass took in pursuit of his goal also teach readers valuable lessons. His success teaches the values of perseverance and faith in one's own abilities.

~~In 1986, The crew of the space shuttle *Challenger* set out to making new discoveries in space. They lost they're lives in a space shuttle disaster. In his speech, "Address to the Nation on the Explosion of the Space Shuttle *Challenger*," President Ronald Reagan reminds Americans that the crew was willed to do a dangerous job. Believing that their mission would be worth the risk.~~

However, failure teaches lessons, too. In 1986, the crew of the space shuttle *Challenger* set out to make new discoveries in space, but they lost their lives in a space shuttle disaster. In his speech "Address to the Nation on the Explosion of the Space Shuttle *Challenger*," President Ronald Reagan reminds Americans that the crew was willing to do a dangerous job. They wanted to travel into space because they believed that the mission would be worth the risk.

And well prepared, there were important questions about the universe that the *Challenger* crew was planning to study. Unfortunately, they never had a chance to acheive that goal because the Space Shuttle exploded after takeoff despite this tragic end, Americans are still to learn a valuable lessen from the *Challenger* crew. Reagan's explaining "The future doesn't belong to the fainthearted; it belongs to the brave. The *Challenger* crew was pulling us into the future, and we'll continue to follow them." The crew was willing to risk their lives to find out new information about the universe. The crew also teaches the values of putting others before yourself and bravery.

~~The risks that you need to take to go after a goal aren't always the same over time. This is evident in "Vanishing Island," an informational article by Anya Groner. In the early 1800s, many members of the Biloxi-Chitimacha-Choctaw Native American tribe established a community on a small island off the coast of Louisiana called Isle de Jean Charles, and it became a "cultural homeland." Since the mid-twentieth century, however, the land on the Island been disappearing into the water that's around the Island at a fast rate. It may not even exist by 2050. As a result, many members of the tribe will risk to give up their land and homes to relocate the community.~~

Skill:
Transitions

Aiko sees that the ideas in the third paragraph do not logically follow from the ideas in the previous paragraph about Frederick Douglass's risk. She searches for a way to use a transition word and a clear topic sentence to show the relationship between the two paragraphs. She uses the linking word "However" to show readers that the outcome of the Challenger crew's risk contrasts with the successful outcome of Frederick Douglass's risk.

Skill:
Style

Aiko starts by looking for sentences that sound conversational, and she finds three issues in her first sentence: It includes a second-person pronoun, the conversational phrase "go after a goal," and a contraction. Since this sentence needs several changes, she decides to rewrite it by using third-person pronouns, replacing the conversational phrase, and avoiding contractions.

 Skill:
Precise Language

Aiko searches for other language that needs to be more specific and vivid. For example, she replaces "wants" with "envisions" and elaborates on the purpose of the museum that the tribal secretary describes.

The risks that one needs to take to pursue a goal can also change over time. This is evident in "The Vanishing Island," an informational article by Anya Groner. In the early 1800s, many members of the Biloxi-Chitimacha-Choctaw Native American tribe established a community on a small island off the coast of Louisiana, and it became a "cultural homeland." The island is called Isle de Jean Charles. Since the mid-twentieth century, however, the land on the island has been rapidly eroding, or wearing away. Storms, river engineering, and pollution are causing this to happen, and the landform may not even exist by 2050.

~~Chief Naquin, the current chief of the Biloxi-Chitimacha-Choctaw Native American tribe, compared the loss of this island to "the loss of a family member." But the members' not giving up and dedicated to preserving their history, community, and culture on the new site. The tribal secretary Chantel Comardelle wants a museum that guides visitor's through the history of the island. Many members of the community also value family. And building houses that give extended families shared backyards. These plans address important issues, but many residents on Isle de Jean Charles will still need to go through a major move, and that teaches readers a lot.~~

Chief Naquin, the current chief of the Biloxi-Chitimacha-Choctaw Native American tribe, compared the loss of this island to "the loss of a family member." Leaving that land will be painful, but members are dedicated to preserving their history, community, and culture on the new site. For example, tribal secretary Chantel Comardelle envisions a museum that guides visitors through the history of the island. Many members of the community also value family. To encourage interactions among family members on the new site, they want to build groups of houses with shared backyards. These plans address important issues, but many residents on Isle de Jean Charles will still need to endure a difficult move. Their sacrifices teach readers the values of determination and resilience, the ability to recover from a loss.

~~People need to consider when risks are worth taking and when they are not worth taken. *Narrative of the Life of Frederick Douglass, An American Slave*, "Address to the Nation on the Explosion of the Space Shuttle *Challenger*," and "Vanishing Island" are stories about~~

~~people who took major risks. The risks that they took were very~~ ~~different, but they all show that risk-taking can help people learn~~ ~~lessons.~~

Narrative of the Life of Frederick Douglass, An American Slave, "Address to the Nation on the Explosion of the Space Shuttle *Challenger*," and "The Vanishing Island" inform readers about historic risks that people have taken to pursue their goals. They show that each person faced hardships as a result of their decisions, and the *Challenger* crew tragically lost their lives. However, their stories continue to teach lessons about honorable qualities. They set examples that readers can follow when they need to decide if they want to take a risk for an important goal.

Skill:
Conclusions

Aiko's revision brings her essay to a close by clearly reviewing her thesis statement and supporting details. To leave her readers with a lasting impression, she also tried to motivate them by adding the final line. It reminds readers that they can use the information in this essay when they need to decide whether or not to take a risk.

Please note that excerpts and passages in the StudySync® library and this workbook are intended as touchstones to generate interest in an author's work. The excerpts and passages do not substitute for the reading of entire texts, and StudySync® strongly recommends that students seek out and purchase the whole literary or informational work in order to experience it as the author intended. Links to online resellers are available in our digital library. In addition, complete works may be ordered through an authorized reseller by filling out and returning to StudySync® the order form enclosed in this workbook.

Reading & Writing
Companion

111

Skill:
Introductions

••• CHECKLIST FOR INTRODUCTIONS

Before you write your introduction, ask yourself the following questions:

- What is my claim?
- How can I introduce my topic clearly?
- How will you "hook" your reader's interest? You might:
  - > start with an attention-grabbing statement
  - > begin with an intriguing question
  - > use descriptive words to set a scene

Below are two strategies to help you introduce your claim and topic clearly in an introduction:

- Peer Discussion
  - > Talk about your topic with a partner, explaining what you already know and your ideas about your topic.
  - > Write notes about the ideas you have discussed and any new questions you may have.
  - > Review your notes and think about what will be your claim or main idea.
  - > Briefly state your claim or thesis statement.
  - > Write ways you can give readers a "preview" of what they will read in the rest of your essay.
  - > Write a possible "hook."

- Freewriting
  - > Freewrite for ten minutes about your topic. Don't worry about grammar, punctuation, or having fully formed ideas. The point of freewriting is to discover ideas.
  - > Review your notes and think about what will be your claim or main idea.
  - > Briefly state your claim or thesis.
  - > Write ways you can give readers a "preview" of what they will read in the rest of your essay.
  - > Write a possible "hook."

Copyright © BookheadEd Learning, LLC

YOUR TURN

Choose the best answer to each question.

1. The following introduction is from a previous draft of Aiko's essay. Aiko would like to replace the underlined sentence with a sentence that better grabs readers' attention and introduces her main idea. Which of these would be the BEST replacement for the underlined sentence?

> <u>Lots of different people take risks.</u> Even if a risk leads to failure, there is always a lesson to learn. There are lessons for the people who have taken the risks, but there are also lessons for people who learn about them. Frederick Douglass, the *Challenger* crew, and the Biloxi-Chitimacha-Choctaw Native American tribe are examples of risk-takers. Their risks and the outcomes of their risks differ, but their stories all teach valuable lessons.

- ○ A. Have you ever taken a risk that didn't work out?
- ○ B. I don't like taking risks.
- ○ C. Sometimes people should not take risks.
- ○ D. Members of the Biloxi-Chitimacha-Choctaw Native American tribe are taking a risk.

2. The following introduction is from a previous draft of Aiko's essay. Aiko would like to replace the underlined sentence with a sentence that explains why she has chosen Frederick Douglass, the *Challenger* crew, and the Biloxi-Chitimacha-Choctaw Native American tribe as examples of risk-takers. Which of these would be the BEST replacement for the underlined sentence?

> Lots of different people take risks. Even if a risk leads to failure, there is always a lesson to learn. There are lessons for the people who have taken the risks, but there are also lessons for people who learn about them. <u>Frederick Douglass, the *Challenger* crew, and the Biloxi-Chitimacha-Choctaw Native American tribe are examples of risk-takers.</u> Their risks and the outcomes of their risks differ, but their stories all teach valuable lessons.

- ○ A. Frederick Douglass, the *Challenger* crew, and the Biloxi-Chitimacha-Choctaw Native American tribe are risk-takers and teachers.
- ○ B. Frederick Douglass, the *Challenger* crew, and the Biloxi-Chitimacha-Choctaw Native American tribe are risk-takers who are noteworthy.
- ○ C. Frederick Douglass, the *Challenger* crew, and the Biloxi-Chitimacha-Choctaw Native American tribe are examples of people who took risks with different outcomes.
- ○ D. Frederick Douglass, the *Challenger* crew, and the Biloxi-Chitimacha-Choctaw Native American tribe are examples of people who took difficult risks for important causes.

Please note that excerpts and passages in the StudySync® library and this workbook are intended as touchstones to generate interest in an author's work. The excerpts and passages do not substitute for the reading of entire texts, and StudySync® strongly recommends that students seek out and purchase the whole literary or informational work in order to experience it as the author intended. Links to online resellers are available in our digital library. In addition, complete works may be ordered through an authorized reseller by filling out and returning to StudySync® the order form enclosed in this workbook.

Reading & Writing Companion   **113**

WRITE

Use the steps in the checklist to revise the introduction of your informative essay.

Skill:
Transitions

••• CHECKLIST FOR TRANSITIONS

Before you revise your current draft to include transitions, think about:

- the key ideas you discuss in your body paragraphs
- how your paragraphs connect together to support your claim(s)
- the relationships among your ideas and concepts
- the logical progression of your ideas

Next, reread your current draft and note areas in your essay where:

- the relationships among your ideas and concepts are unclear, identifying places where you could add linking words or other transitional devices to make your essay more cohesive. Look for:

  > sudden jumps in your ideas

  > breaks between paragraphs where the ideas in the next paragraph are not logically following from the previous one

Revise your draft to use words, phrases, and clauses to create cohesion and clarify the relationships among your ideas and concepts, using the following questions as a guide:

- Are there unifying relationships between the ideas I present in my essay?
- Have I clarified, or made clear, these relationships?
- What linking words (such as conjunctions), phrases, or clauses could I add to my essay to clarify the relationships among the ideas and concepts I present?

⟳ YOUR TURN

Choose the best answer to each question.

1. Below is an excerpt from a previous draft of Aiko's informative essay. Aiko notices that her introduction and first body paragraphs are not clearly connected to one another, so she wants to revise the underlined sentence. Which of the following sentences clearly shows how the main idea of the first body paragraph relates to the topic of the essay?

> Frederick Douglass, the crew of the *Challenger*, and members of the Biloxi-Chitimacha-Choctaw Native American tribe all risked losses in pursuit of their goals. Even though their risks and the outcomes of their risks differ, they all required courage.
>
> <u>Douglass describes a major risk that he took in his autobiography.</u> Born into slavery, Douglass was legally denied an education. At first, his mistress started teaching him how to read, but after she changed her mind about teaching him, she became angry and violent when he tried to learn on his own.

○ A. In Frederick Douglass's autobiography, Douglass described how he learned to read and write while risking severe punishment.

○ B. In Frederick Douglass's autobiography, Douglass described his effort to learn how to read and write, and the outcome of this risk was positive.

○ C. As an example, Frederick Douglass described major risks that he took while learning how to read and write.

○ D. As an example, Frederick Douglass wrote about acts of courage in his autobiography.

2. Below is a body paragraph from a previous draft of Aiko's informative essay. Aiko would like to add a transition word or phrase to help readers move from sentence 2 to sentence 3. Which transition will work best?

> (1) Risks can also have tragic outcomes. (2) For example, the space shuttle *Challenger* exploded after takeoff in 1986. (3) After the disaster occurred, President Reagan reflected on this tragedy in his speech "Address to the Nation on the Explosion of the Space Shuttle *Challenger*." (4) He mourned the loss of the crew and emphasized that their risks took great courage. (5) He said, "And perhaps we've forgotten the courage it took for the crew of the shuttle. (6) But they, the *Challenger* Seven, were aware of the dangers, but overcame them and did their jobs brilliantly."

○ A. Similarly,

○ B. For example,

○ C. In addition to that detail,

○ D. As a result,

WRITE

Use the questions in the checklist to revise one of your body paragraphs. Look for a variety of ways to use words, phrases, and clauses to create cohesion and clarify the relationships among ideas in this section. Those ideas may include your claim, counterclaims, reasons, and evidence.

Please note that excerpts and passages in the StudySync® library and this workbook are intended as touchstones to generate interest in an author's work. The excerpts and passages do not substitute for the reading of entire texts, and StudySync® strongly recommends that students seek out and purchase the whole literary or informational work in order to experience it as the author intended. Links to online resellers are available in our digital library. In addition, complete works may be ordered through an authorized reseller by filling out and returning to StudySync® the order form enclosed in this workbook.

Reading & Writing Companion

117

Skill:
Precise Language

••• CHECKLIST FOR PRECISE LANGUAGE

As you consider precise language and domain-specific vocabulary related to a subject or topic, use the following questions as a guide:

- What information am I trying to convey or explain to my audience?
- Are there any key concepts that need to be explained or understood?
- What domain-specific vocabulary is relevant to my topic and explanation?
- Where can I use more precise vocabulary in my explanation?

Here are some suggestions that will help guide you in using precise language and domain-specific vocabulary to inform about or explain a topic:

- Determine the topic or area of study you will be writing about.
- Identify key concepts that need explanation in order to inform readers.
- Research any domain-specific vocabulary that you may need to define.
- Substitute precise, descriptive, and domain-specific language for vague, general, or overused words and phrases.
- Reread your writing to refine and revise if needed.

↻ YOUR TURN

Choose the best answer to each question.

1. Aiko wants to improve the underlined sentence from a previous draft that included a paragraph about "The Day I Saved a Life." How can she use domain-specific vocabulary and more precise language in the underlined sentence?

> In "The Day I Saved a Life," Thomas Ponce took a risk by dedicating himself to protecting a shark. Due to their roles in horror movies like *Jaws*, sharks are often seen as evil predators who do not need to be saved. <u>However, Ponce pointed out that sharks are necessary in the ocean, and they are often hurt by human beings.</u> He used that knowledge to speak on behalf of a shark that a fisherman had caught, and Ponce saved the shark's life as a result. That risk took courage because Ponce decided to do something difficult that needed to be done quickly.

- ○ A. However, Ponce informs readers that sharks are needed in oceans, and human beings often cause harm to them.
- ○ B. However, Ponce adds that they are very important in the ocean, and they are often unnecessarily removed from it or hurt by human beings.
- ○ C. However, Ponce says that sharks are absolutely necessary in the ocean, and they are often the victims.
- ○ D. However, Ponce explains that sharks are vital parts of their ecosystems, and they are often victims of cruelty by human beings.

2. Aiko wants to improve the underlined sentence from one of her previous drafts by revising and refining the language. How can she use more precise language in the underlined sentence?

> In "The Day I Saved a Life," Thomas Ponce took a risk by dedicating himself to protecting a shark. Due to their roles in horror movies like *Jaws*, sharks are often seen as evil predators who do not need to be saved. However, Ponce pointed out that sharks are necessary in the ocean, and they are often hurt by human beings. He used that knowledge to speak on behalf of a shark that a fisherman had caught, and Ponce saved the shark's life as a result. <u>That risk took courage because Ponce decided to do something difficult that needed to be done quickly.</u>

- ○ A. That risk took courage because Ponce took action, and he could have done nothing instead.
- ○ B. That risk took courage because the situation was urgent, and Ponce's goal was difficult to achieve.
- ○ C. That risk took courage because Ponce could have failed to do something difficult.
- ○ D. That risk took courage because it involved a shark and someone else achieving his goal of catching that shark.

Please note that excerpts and passages in the StudySync® library and this workbook are intended as touchstones to generate interest in an author's work. The excerpts and passages do not substitute for the reading of entire texts, and StudySync® strongly recommends that students seek out and purchase the whole literary or informational work in order to experience it as the author intended. Links to online resellers are available in our digital library. In addition, complete works may be ordered through an authorized reseller by filling out and returning to StudySync® the order form enclosed in this workbook.

Reading & Writing Companion   119

YOUR TURN

Identify at least five sentences from your draft that need more precise language and write them in the first column. Then, complete the chart by writing a revised sentence in the second column.

Draft Sentence	Revised Sentence

Skill:
Style

STYLE

sync•skill

••• CHECKLIST FOR STYLE

First, reread the draft of your informative essay and identify the following:

- places where you use slang, contractions, abbreviations, and a conversational tone

- areas where you could use subject-specific or academic language in order to help persuade or inform your readers

- moments where you use first person (*I*) or second person (*you*)

- areas where sentence structure lacks variety

- incorrect uses of the conventions of standard English for grammar, spelling, capitalization, and punctuation

Establish and maintain a formal style in your essay, using the following questions as a guide:

- Have I avoided slang in favor of academic language?

- Did I consistently use a third-person point of view, using third-person pronouns (*he*, *she*, *they*)?

- Have I varied my sentence structure and the length of my sentences? Apply these specific questions where appropriate:

  > Where should I make some sentences longer by using conjunctions to connect independent clauses, dependent clauses, and phrases?

  > Where should I make some sentences shorter by separating any independent clauses?

- Did I follow the conventions of standard English, including:

  > grammar?

  > spelling?

  > capitalization?

  > punctuation?

Please note that excerpts and passages in the StudySync® library and this workbook are intended as touchstones to generate interest in an author's work. The excerpts and passages do not substitute for the reading of entire texts, and StudySync® strongly recommends that students seek out and purchase the whole literary or informational work in order to experience it as the author intended. Links to online resellers are available in our digital library. In addition, complete works may be ordered through an authorized reseller by filling out and returning to StudySync® the order form enclosed in this workbook.

Reading & Writing Companion

121

YOUR TURN

Choose the best answer to each question.

1. Below is a section from a previous draft of Aiko's informative essay. She sees that she needs to revise the language in the underlined sentence to make sure that it is written in a formal style. Which of the following sentences is a successful revision that is written in a formal style?

> A resettlement committee is working on a design for the new site, and their plan should help the community achieve their goals. To preserve the community's history on Isle de Jean Charles, the site may include a museum. It'd guide us through information about the island and what it was like to live on it. Many members of the community also value family, and they'd like to build houses that give extended families a shared backyard.

○ A. It would guide you through information about the island and what it was like to live on it.

○ B. It guides you through information about the island and what it was like to live on it.

○ C. It would guide visitors through information about the island and the community's experiences on it.

○ D. It guides visitors through information about the island and the communitys experiences on it.

2. Below is a section from a previous draft of Aiko's informative essay. Aiko wants to vary the length of her sentences, so she decides to rewrite the underlined sentence as two separate independent clauses. Which of the following sentences successfully divide the underlined sentence into separate independent clauses that are written in a formal style?

> A resettlement committee is working on a design for the new site, and their plan should help the community achieve their goals. To preserve the community's history on Isle de Jean Charles, the site may include a museum. It'd guide us through information about the island and what it was like to live on it. Many members of the community also value family, and they'd like to build houses that give extended families a shared backyard.

○ A. Many members of the community also value family and would like to build houses for them. They'll give extended families a shared backyard.

○ B. Many members of the community also value family and would like to build houses for them. Giving extended families backyards to share.

○ C. Many members of the community also value family. And they would like to build houses that give extended families a shared backyard.

○ D. Many members of the community also value family. For this reason, they would like to build houses that give extended families a shared backyard.

WRITE

Use the steps in the checklist to add to or revise the language of one paragraph from your draft by establishing and maintaining a formal style.

Skill:
Conclusions

••• CHECKLIST FOR CONCLUSIONS

Before you write your conclusion, ask yourself the following questions:

- How can I restate the thesis or main idea in my concluding section or statement? What impression can I make on my reader?

- How can I write my conclusion so that it supports and follows logically from my argument?

- How can I conclude with a memorable comment?

Below are two strategies to help you provide a concluding statement or section that follows from and supports the argument presented:

- Peer Discussion

  > After you have written your introduction and body paragraphs, talk with a partner and tell him or her what you want readers to remember, writing notes about your discussion.

  > Review your notes and think about what you wish to express in your conclusion.

  > Do not simply restate your claim or thesis statement. Rephrase your main idea to show the depth of your knowledge and the importance of your idea.

  > Write your conclusion.

- Freewriting

  > Freewrite for ten minutes about what you might include in your conclusion. Don't worry about grammar, punctuation, or having fully formed ideas. The point of freewriting is to discover ideas.

  > Review your notes and think about what you wish to express in your conclusion.

  > Do not simply restate your claim or thesis statement. Rephrase your main idea to show the depth of your knowledge and the importance of your idea.

  > Write your conclusion.

⟳ YOUR TURN

Choose the best answer to each question.

1. The following conclusion is from a previous draft of Aiko's essay. Aiko sees that she copied the thesis statement from the introduction and pasted it at the end of her conclusion. As a result, she would like to rephrase the underlined sentence so that it engages readers. Which of the following sentences would be the BEST replacement for the underlined sentence?

> Frederick Douglass, the *Challenger* crew, and members of the Biloxi-Chitimacha-Choctaw Native American tribe all took risks to pursue important goals. Frederick Douglass found ways to learn how to read and write even though it was illegal for him to get an education at the time. The *Challenger* crew wanted to explore space, but they lost their lives just after their shuttle took off. Members of the Biloxi-Chitimacha-Choctaw Native American tribe wanted to reestablish their homes and culture on new land, and the outcome of their work was not known when "Vanishing Island" was published. <u>Even though these risks and their outcomes differ, they all teach essential lessons.</u>

- ○ A. These risks and their outcomes vary widely, but they all teach valuable lessons.
- ○ B. It is also evident that every risk teaches readers a valuable lesson.
- ○ C. Readers can learn valuable lessons from each risk.
- ○ D. These are the risks that each person took to pursue an important goal.

2. The following conclusion is from a previous draft of Aiko's essay. Aiko would like to add a sentence to bring her essay to a more effective close. Which sentence could she add after the last sentence to help achieve this goal?

> Frederick Douglass, the *Challenger* crew, and members of the Biloxi-Chitimacha-Choctaw Native American tribe all took risks to pursue important goals. Frederick Douglass found ways to learn how to read and write even though it was illegal for him to get an education at the time. The *Challenger* crew wanted to explore space, but they lost their lives just after their shuttle took off. Members of the Biloxi-Chitimacha-Choctaw Native American tribe wanted to reestablish their homes and culture on new land, and the outcome of their work was not known when "Vanishing Island" was published. Even though these risks and their outcomes differ, they all teach essential lessons.

- ○ A. The lesson from the Biloxi-Chitimacha-Choctaw Native American tribe is the most recent example.
- ○ B. What is an example of a lesson that you learned from each selection?
- ○ C. I think that the lessons I learned from each story apply to my life and my classmates' lives as well.
- ○ D. Each story shows readers personal qualities that everyone can work to develop.

WRITE

Use the steps in the checklist to revise the conclusion of your informative essay.

Informative Writing Process: Revise

PLAN	DRAFT	REVISE	EDIT AND PUBLISH

You have written a draft of your informative essay. You have also received input from your peers about how to improve it. Now you are going to revise your draft.

← REVISION GUIDE

Examine your draft to find areas for revision. Keep in mind your purpose and audience as you revise for clarity, development, organization, and style. Use the guide below to help you review:

Review	Revise	Example
Clarity		
Identify the information you want to convey and any concepts that need to be explained. Annotate places where you can add domain-specific vocabulary to clarify information or explain a concept.	Clarify information or explain a concept by using domain-specific vocabulary. Remember to think about whether or not you need to define a term for your audience.	Since the mid-twentieth century, however, the land on the island has been rapidly eroding, or wearing away. It Storms, river engineering, and pollution are causing this to happen, and the landform may not even exist by 2050.

Please note that excerpts and passages in the StudySync® library and this workbook are intended as touchstones to generate interest in an author's work. The excerpts and passages do not substitute for the reading of entire texts, and StudySync® strongly recommends that students seek out and purchase the whole literary or informational work in order to experience it as the author intended. Links to online resellers are available in our digital library. In addition, complete works may be ordered through an authorized reseller by filling out and returning to StudySync® the order form enclosed in this workbook.

Reading & Writing Companion   **127**

Review	Revise	Example
Development		
Identify your main idea about the topic. Annotate places where you need to add, replace, or remove supporting details. Each detail should clearly help develop the main idea.	Make sure to include textual evidence from the selections that you have read, and use quotation marks when you are quoting a source directly.	In his speech "Address to the Nation on the Explosion of the Space Shuttle *Challenger*," President Ronald Reagan reminds Americans that the crew was willing to do a dangerous job. They wanted to travel into space because they believed that the mission would be worth the risk. He says, "They had a hunger to explore the universe and discover its truths."
Organization		
Review your body paragraphs. Identify and annotate any sentences that don't flow in a clear and logical way.	Rewrite the sentences so that the information flows from one idea to another. Make sure that you have clearly expressed the relationships between ideas.	Leaving that land will be painful. ~~On the new site~~, but members are dedicated to preserving their history, community, and culture on the new site. ~~The~~ For example, tribal secretary Chantel Comardelle envisions a museum that guides visitors through the history of the island.
Style: Word Choice		
Identify weak or repetitive words or phrases that do not clearly express your ideas to the reader.	Replace weak and repetitive words and phrases with more descriptive ones that better convey your ideas.	The crew was willing to risk their lives ~~to find out new information~~ in search of knowledge about the universe. ~~The crew also~~ Their efforts teach the values of ~~putting others before yourself~~ selflessness and bravery.

Review	Revise	Example
Style: Sentence Variety		
Read your informative essay aloud. Annotate places where you have too many long or short sentences in a row.	Revise short sentences by linking them together. Shorten longer sentences for clarity of emphasis.	Many members of the community also value family;. To encourage interactions among family members on the new site, ~~so~~ they want to build groups of houses with shared backyards.

✏ WRITE

Use the guide above, as well as your peer reviews, to help you evaluate your informative essay to determine areas that should be revised.

Grammar: Participles

A present participle is formed by adding *-ing* to a verb. As part of a verb phrase, the present participle is used with forms of the helping verb *to be*.

A past participle is usually formed by adding *-ed* to a verb. The past participle of some verbs has other endings, as in *broken*. When a participle acts as the main verb in a verb phrase, it is used with forms of the helping verb *to have*.

A present or past participle can also act as an adjective to describe, or modify, a noun or a pronoun. When a participle acts as an adjective, it is called a verbal.

Participle as a Verb	Participle as an Adjective
They looked the same as the other people from Africa who had been **coming** over, who had dark skin. The People Could Fly: American Black Folktales	A poor, bare, miserable room it was, with **broken** windows, no fire, ragged bedclothes, a sick mother, **wailing** baby, and a group of pale, hungry children **cuddled** under one old quilt, **trying** to keep warm. Little Women

Both present and past participles can function as either verbs or adjectives.

Text	Function	Explanation
But Coach had **spoken**, and his word was law on the court. Middle School Madness	verb	**Spoken** is a past participle. It works with the helping verb *had* to tell what *Coach* had done.
The magical time of childhood stood still, and the pulse of the **living** earth pressed its mystery into my **living** blood. A Celebration of Grandfathers	adjective	**Living** is a present participle. It modifies the nouns *earth* and *blood*.

↻ YOUR TURN

1. Choose the revision that uses a participle as an adjective.

> The sun rises slowly, and its light spreads along the horizon.

- ○ A. The sun rises slowly, and its light is spreading along the horizon.
- ○ B. The sun has been rising slowly, and its light spreads along the horizon.
- ○ C. The rising sun spreads light slowly along the horizon.
- ○ D. No change needs to be made to this sentence.

2. Choose the revision that uses a participle as an adjective.

> Ruby struggled to sleep through the sound of the crickets that chirped all night.

- ○ A. Ruby struggled to sleep through the sound of the crickets that were chirping all night.
- ○ B. All night, Ruby struggled to sleep through the sound of the chirping crickets.
- ○ C. Ruby was struggling to sleep through the sound of the crickets that chirped all night.
- ○ D. No change needs to be made to this sentence.

3. Choose the revision that uses a participle as an adjective.

> The Civil War challenged Americans and reshaped their ideas about freedom.

- ○ A. The Civil War was challenging to Americans and reshaped their ideas about freedom.
- ○ B. The Civil War is challenging to Americans and has been reshaping their ideas about freedom.
- ○ C. The Civil War was a challenging time for Americans and reshaped their ideas about freedom.
- ○ D. No change needs to be made to this sentence.

Grammar: Gerunds

A gerund is a noun that is formed from the present participle of a verb.

A present participle is formed by adding *-ing* to the base form of a verb. When used as verbs, present participles always follow a form of the verb *to be* (for example, *We are going to the car*). Without a helping verb, present participles can be used as adjectives.

The way a present participle is used in a sentence determines if it is a gerund. A gerund can be the subject of a sentence, the direct object of a verb, or the object of a preposition.

Text	Explanation
High in the crow's-nest of the New White Star Liner Titanic, Lookout Frederick Fleet peered into a **dazzling** night. A Night to Remember	*Dazzling* is the present participle of the verb *to dazzle*. Here it is used as an adjective modifying the noun *night*.
"Yes," I replied, answering for her, "I paid her for everything, and the **eating** was the worst I ever tried." Ten Days in a Mad-House	The gerund *eating* is used as the subject of the last main clause. Note that *answering* is part of the participial phrase *answering for her*, used as an adjective modifying *I*.
He never stopped **growling**. Cujo	The gerund *growling* is used as the direct object of the verb *stopped*.
The **ringing** became more distinct: it continued and became more distinct; I talked more freely to get rid of the feeling: but it continued and gained definitiveness--until, at length, I found that the noise was *not* within my ears. The Tell-Tale Heart	The gerund *ringing* is the subject of the verb *became*.

↻ YOUR TURN

1. Replace the words in bold with a gerund.

> A study by six leading medical organizations concludes that "**to view** entertainment violence can lead to an increase in aggressive attitudes, values, and behavior, particularly in children."

- ○ A. viewer
- ○ B. viewing
- ○ C. viewed
- ○ D. None of the above

2. Replace the word in bold with a gerund.

> The young man's **cope** with impossible situations such as those in the Japanese internment camps took an amazing amount of strength along with a positive attitude.

- ○ A. coping
- ○ B. coped
- ○ C. is coping
- ○ D. None of the above

3. Replace the word in bold with a gerund.

> I think Reanna is training to be a spy—no one could be more discreet in **deliver** secret messages!

- ○ A. delivers
- ○ B. delivered
- ○ C. delivering
- ○ D. None of the above

4. Replace the words in bold with a gerund.

> Mia prefers **to read** about real-life unsolved mysteries, while most of her friends choose to read mind-bending science fiction or engaging crime novels.

- ○ A. reading
- ○ B. to read
- ○ C. has read
- ○ D. None of the above

Grammar: Infinitives

The function of a verb is to name an action or state of being, or to describe "having." An infinitive is a verb form that may function as a noun, an adjective, or an adverb. An infinitive is formed from the word *to* followed by the base form of a verb. The word *to* is not a preposition when it is used immediately before a verb.

An infinitive used as a noun can be the subject of a sentence or the direct object of a verb.

Infinitives Are Not Prepositions	Example
When the word *to* appears before a noun or a pronoun, it is a preposition. When *to* appears before the base form of a verb, the two words form an infinitive.	Then, miraculously, the bow began **to swing** to port. A Night to Remember

Infinitives Used as Nouns	Example
The infinitive can be the subject of a sentence.	**To resist** takes courage.
The infinitive can be the direct object of a verb.	The prisoners decided **to resist**.

Infinitives Used as Adjectives or Adverbs	Example
The infinitive can be used as an adjective to modify a noun or a pronoun.	"That's the worst of living so far out," bawled Mr. White, with sudden and unlooked-for violence; "of all the beastly, slushy, out-of-the-way places **to live** in, this is the worst. . . ." The Monkey's Paw
The infinitive can be used as an adverb to modify a verb, an adjective, or another adverb.	But I guess she deserves some kind of award for having had ten kids and survived **to tell** about it. Abuela Invents the Zero

⟳ YOUR TURN

1. Identify the infinitive in this sentence.

   > We went to the park to find the bench that she usually went to when she needed time to herself.

   ○ A. to the park
   ○ B. to find
   ○ C. to herself
   ○ D. There is no infinitive in this sentence.

2. Identify the infinitive in this sentence.

   > To develop her ear for music, she went to as many free concerts as possible, while also adhering to her daily practice schedule.

   ○ A. To develop
   ○ B. to as many
   ○ C. to her daily practice schedule
   ○ D. There is no infinitive in this sentence.

3. Identify the infinitive in this sentence.

   > From eight to ten candidates have registered to participate in the debates that have been assigned to Ellen for scheduling.

   ○ A. to ten
   ○ B. to participate
   ○ C. to Ellen
   ○ D. There is no infinitive in this sentence.

4. Identify the infinitive in this sentence.

   > Why would I bow to her demand for another cake to serve when she did not invite me to the party?

   ○ A. to her demand
   ○ B. to serve
   ○ C. to the party
   ○ D. There is no infinitive in this sentence.

Please note that excerpts and passages in the StudySync® library and this workbook are intended as touchstones to generate interest in an author's work. The excerpts and passages do not substitute for the reading of entire texts, and StudySync® strongly recommends that students seek out and purchase the whole literary or informational work in order to experience it as the author intended. Links to online resellers are available in our digital library. In addition, complete works may be ordered through an authorized reseller by filling out and returning to StudySync® the order form enclosed in this workbook.

Reading & Writing Companion   135

Informative Writing Process: Edit and Publish

| PLAN | DRAFT | REVISE | EDIT AND PUBLISH |

You have revised your informative essay based on your peer feedback and your own examination.

Now, it is time to edit your informative essay. When you revised, you focused on the content of your informative essay. You probably looked at your essay's introduction, supporting ideas, and conclusion. When you edit, you focus on the mechanics of your essay, paying close attention to things like grammar and punctuation.

Use the checklist below to guide you as you edit:

☐ Have I used participles correctly?

☐ Have I used gerunds correctly?

☐ Have I used infinitives correctly?

☐ Do I have any sentence fragments or run-on sentences?

☐ Have I spelled everything correctly?

Notice some edits Aiko has made:

• Rewrote a sentence with a participle that did not clearly describe a noun, adjective, or adverb.

• Corrected a spelling mistake.

• Fixed a run-on sentence by dividing it into two separate sentences.

• Replaced an infinitive that did not make sense with a verb.

• Fixed a sentence fragment by replacing a gerund with a verb.

~~And~~ The *Challenger* crew was well prepared~~, there were important questions about the universe that the *Challenger* crew was~~ and planning to study important questions about the universe. Unfortunately, they never had a chance to ~~acheive~~ achieve that goal because the space shuttle exploded after takeoff ~~despite~~. Despite this tragic end, Americans can ~~are~~ still ~~to~~ learn a valuable ~~lessen~~ lesson from the *Challenger* crew. Reagan~~'s explaining~~ explains that "the future doesn't belong to the fainthearted; it belongs to the brave. The *Challenger* crew was pulling us into the future, and we'll continue to follow them." The crew was willing to risk their lives in search of knowledge about the universe. Their efforts teach the values of selflessness and bravery.

✏ WRITE

Use the questions on the previous page, as well as your peer reviews, to help you evaluate your informative essay to determine areas that need editing. Then edit your essay to correct those errors.

Once you have made all your corrections, you are ready to publish your work. You can distribute your writing to family and friends, hang it on a bulletin board, or post it on your blog. If you publish online, share the link with your family, friends, and classmates.

Please note that excerpts and passages in the StudySync® library and this workbook are intended as touchstones to generate interest in an author's work. The excerpts and passages do not substitute for the reading of entire texts, and StudySync® strongly recommends that students seek out and purchase the whole literary or informational work in order to experience it as the author intended. Links to online resellers are available in our digital library. In addition, complete works may be ordered through an authorized reseller by filling out and returning to StudySync® the order form enclosed in this workbook.

Reading & Writing Companion   **137**

The History of the Space Shuttle

INFORMATIONAL TEXT

Introduction

Through great achievements and heartbreaking losses, NASA's Space Shuttles and the crews that flew them into space and back captured America's hearts and minds. The Space Shuttle was a reusable vehicle that allowed NASA to carry out 135 missions as well as send more than 350 people and 3 million pounds of cargo into space. Although the program ended in 2011, its triumphs and tragedies remain an important part of American history.

V VOCABULARY

satellite
an object that follows a consistent course around a larger object

fleet
a group of vehicles that are owned and operated by the same company

orbit
to revolve around a large object in a curved path

disintegrate
to fall apart or separate into pieces

clear
to approve or give official permission

≡ READ

NOTES

1   The Space Shuttle program ran for three decades and 135 missions. It launched more than 350 people and 3 million pounds of cargo into space. Some of these missions ended in joyful celebrations. Others led to tragedy. Overall, the Space Shuttle program was an impressive achievement.

2   The National Aeronautics and Space Administration (NASA) was founded in 1958. Americans wanted to enter the Space Race. The Soviet Union launched the world's first made-man **satellite** in 1957. Interest in space exploration grew. In 1962, President John F. Kennedy said that NASA would put a man on the Moon. On July 20, 1969, Neil Armstrong achieved that goal.

3   With the success of the Moon landing behind them, NASA's scientists needed a new goal. A task force wanted to design a reusable space vehicle. They also wanted to build a space station and launch missions to Mars. President Richard Nixon told them to focus on the vehicle. The Space Shuttle program was born.

4   Each shuttle has three main parts. The orbiter is the astronauts' home in space. There are two solid rocket boosters (SRBs). The SRBs create the force needed to launch. They break off. The last piece of the puzzle is the external fuel tank (ET). The ET provides fuel for launch. It also separates. The orbiter carries fuel for the mission and reentry.

5   The first shuttle, *Enterprise*, was never **cleared** for space. In April 1981, *Columbia* **orbited** the Earth 37 times before its arrival home. *Challenger* was built in 1983. *Discovery* followed in 1984. *Atlantis* joined the **fleet** a year later. With many successes under their belt, NASA had a failure. The shuttles were not reliable. On January 28, 1986, *Challenger* exploded 73 seconds after liftoff. The crew was killed. The likelihood of the disaster seemed low. America wept. NASA didn't launch another mission for two years.

6   The Space Shuttle program continued. *Challenger's* replacement, *Endeavour*, was built in 1992. The shuttles' crews worked to put satellites into orbit. They launched and repaired the Hubble Space Telescope. They worked on the International Space Station.

7   Another tragedy struck on February 1, 2003. *Columbia* **disintegrated** coming back to Earth. The crew was killed. The loss shook the nation. The program carried on.

8   The end of the historic Space Shuttle program was announced in 2004. NASA's budget grew smaller. Its priorities changed. The orbiters and SRBs were reusable, but they were expensive to maintain. The final mission ended on July 21, 2011. *Atlantis* landed safely. It joined the other shuttles in retirement.

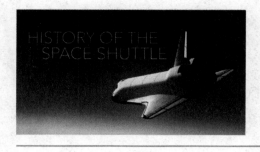

First Read

Read the text. After you read, answer the Think Questions below.

☁ THINK QUESTIONS

1. When and why was NASA founded?

   NASA was founded in _____.

   It was founded because _____.

2. What are the parts of a Space Shuttle?

   The parts of the Space Shuttle are _____

   _____.

3. What type of work did crews use Space Shuttles to do?

   Crews used the Space Shuttle to _____

   _____.

4. Use context to confirm the meaning of the word *fleet* as it is used in "The History of the Space Shuttle." Write your definition of *fleet* here.

   Fleet means _____.

   A context clue is _____.

5. What is another way to say that someone has *cleared* a plan?

   Someone has _____.

Copyright © BookheadEd Learning, LLC

Skill:
Analyzing Expressions

★ DEFINE

When you read, you may find English expressions that you do not know. An **expression** is a group of words that communicates an idea. Three types of expressions are idioms, sayings, and figurative language. They can be difficult to understand because the meanings of the words are different from their **literal**, or usual, meanings.

An idiom is an expression that is commonly known among a group of people. For example: "It's raining cats and dogs" means it is raining heavily. **Sayings** are short expressions that contain advice or wisdom. For instance: "Don't count your chickens before they hatch" means do not plan on something good happening before it happens. **Figurative** language is when you describe something by comparing it with something else, either directly (using the words *like* or *as*) or indirectly. For example, "I'm as hungry as a horse" means I'm very hungry. None of the expressions are about actual animals.

••• CHECKLIST FOR ANALYZING EXPRESSIONS

To determine the meaning of an expression, remember the following:

✓ If you find a confusing group of words, it may be an expression. The meaning of words in expressions may not be their literal meaning.

- Ask yourself: Is this confusing because the words are new? Or because the words do not make sense together?

✓ Determining the overall meaning may require that you use one or more of the following:

- context clues

- a dictionary or other resource

- teacher or peer support

✓ Highlight important information before and after the expression to look for clues.

⟳ YOUR TURN

Read paragraphs 4–7 from the text. Then, complete the multiple-choice questions below.

---

from **"The History of the Space Shuttle"**

Each shuttle has three main parts. The orbiter is the astronauts' home in space. There are two solid rocket boosters (SRBs). The SRBs create the force needed to launch. They break off. The last piece of the puzzle is the external fuel tank (ET). The ET provides fuel for launch. It also separates. The orbiter carries fuel for the mission and reentry.

The first shuttle, *Enterprise*, was never cleared for space. In April 1981, *Columbia* orbited the Earth 37 times before its arrival home. *Challenger* was built in 1983. *Discovery* followed in 1984. *Atlantis* joined the fleet a year later. With many successes under their belt, NASA had a failure. The shuttles were not reliable. On January 28, 1986, *Challenger* exploded 73 seconds after liftoff. The crew was killed. The likelihood of the disaster seemed low. America wept. NASA didn't launch another mission for two years.

The Space Shuttle program continued. *Challenger's* replacement, *Endeavour*, was built in 1992. The shuttles' crews worked to put satellites into orbit. They launched and repaired the Hubble Space Telescope. They worked on the International Space Station.

Another tragedy struck on February 1, 2003. *Columbia* disintegrated coming back to Earth. The crew was killed. The loss shook the nation. The program carried on.

---

1. In paragraph 4, the sentence "The last piece of the puzzle is the external fuel tank (ET)" means that the ET:

   ○ A. was hard to put together.

   ○ B. had a lot of parts.

   ○ C. was part of the shuttle.

   ○ D. was hard to understand.

2. In paragraph 5, the phrase "With many successes under their belt" means that NASA:

   ○ A. got new uniforms.

   ○ B. had many achievements.

   ○ C. made a mistake.

   ○ D. discovered an asteroid belt.

3. In paragraph 5, the sentence "America wept" means that Americans felt:

    ○ A. sad.
    ○ B. mad.
    ○ C. joyful.
    ○ D. surprised.

4. In paragraph 7, the sentence "The loss shook the nation" means that Americans:

    ○ A. had an earthquake.
    ○ B. had a strong reaction.
    ○ C. did not support NASA.
    ○ D. felt strong winds.

Skill:
Main Ideas and Details

★ DEFINE

The **main ideas** are the most important ideas of a paragraph, a section, or an entire text. The **supporting details** are details that describe or explain the main idea.

To **distinguish** between the main ideas and the supporting details, you will need to decide what information is the most important and supports or explains the main ideas.

••• CHECKLIST FOR MAIN IDEAS AND DETAILS

In order to distinguish between main ideas and supporting details, do the following:

✓ Preview the text. Look at headings, topic sentences, and boldface vocabulary.

  • Ask yourself: What seem to be the main ideas in this text?

✓ Read the text.

  • Ask yourself: What are the most important ideas? What details support or explain the most important ideas?

✓ Take notes or use a graphic organizer to distinguish between main ideas and supporting details.

YOUR TURN

Read paragraphs 7–8 from the text. Then, complete the multiple-choice questions below.

---

from **"The History of the Space Shuttle"**

Another tragedy struck on February 1, 2003. *Columbia* disintegrated coming back to Earth. The crew was killed. The loss shook the nation. The program carried on.

The end of the historic Space Shuttle program was announced in 2004. NASA's budget grew smaller. Its priorities changed. The orbiters and SRBs were reusable, but they were expensive to maintain. The final mission ended on July 21, 2011. Atlantis landed safely. It joined the other shuttles in retirement.

---

1. The main idea of paragraph 7 is that NASA:

    ○ A. kept going.
    ○ B. had an accident.
    ○ C. was shocked.
    ○ D. did not know what to do.

2. A supporting detail that best develops this main idea is:

    ○ A. "Another tragedy struck on February 1, 2003."
    ○ B. "*Columbia* disintegrated coming back to Earth."
    ○ C. "The loss shook the nation."
    ○ D. "The program carried on."

3. The main idea of paragraph 8 is that the Space Shuttle program:

    ○ A. was expensive.
    ○ B. reused some parts.
    ○ C. had many shuttles.
    ○ D. came to an end.

4. A supporting detail that best develops this main idea is:

    ○ A. "NASA's budget grew smaller. Its priorities changed."
    ○ B. "The orbiters and SRBs were reusable, but they were expensive to maintain."
    ○ C. "The final mission ended on July 21, 2011."
    ○ D. "Atlantis landed safely."

Close Read

 WRITE

ARGUMENTATIVE: Should NASA restart the Space Shuttle program? Why or why not? Write a short paragraph in which you state your opinion on this topic. Support your claim with details from the text. Pay attention to correctly spelling words with suffixes as you write.

Use the checklist below to guide you as you write.

☐ Do you think NASA should restart the Space Shuttle program?

☐ Why do you feel that way?

☐ What details in the text support your opinion?

Use the sentence frames to organize and write your argument.

NASA (should / should not) restart the Space Shuttle program.

Restarting the Space Shuttle program would be _____.

I think this because _____.

Overall, the Space Shuttle program was _____,

but it was also _____.

Details that support this opinion are _____ and _____.

Narrative of the Life of Ada Lee

FICTION

Introduction

The title of "Narrative of the Life of Ada Lee, an American Farm Girl" hints at the autobiography *Narrative of the Life of Frederick Douglass, an American Slave*. This work of historical fiction makes connections between Douglass's efforts to educate himself despite laws that forbade slaves from doing so and Ada's own struggle to pursue a career despite legal and cultural unfairness to women.

 VOCABULARY

secret
known by only a few people

earnest
sincere and serious

enroll
to register for or enter

grieving
to feel deep sadness

incomprehensible
unable to be understood

≡ READ

NOTES

1   I sat down on the stool and dug my heels into the barn's dirt floor. "You know I love you, Bessie," I whispered dreamily to our dairy cow, "but I'm not going to be with you for much longer. I am going to college." A **secret** grin spread slowly across my face. It was the first time I had said my plan out loud. "I know what you're thinking, Bessie," I continued, patting her gently. Women could not go to college, but I had heard about a college on the east coast that would accept female students. The school was far away. The workload might be very hard, given my limited education. But I was determined to **enroll**. After all, I had taught myself to read. Learning from a teacher couldn't be harder than that. "It's going to be hard, but I will go to school and become a lawyer."

2   College was different than I had expected it to be. I missed my life on the farm, and the pile of books that rested on my desk practically reached the ceiling. They were filled with **incomprehensible** legal terminology that I hadn't much use for back home. I knew I needed to get some help if I were to

succeed. John Wilson was a young man in the law program who came from a long line of lawyers. One day, I flashed John a smile and told him I'd exchange home-cooked meals for some tutoring. He gladly accepted.

3   John and I worked together from then on. By the time we had earned our law degrees, we had grown quite close. We were married after graduation. It was my **earnest** wish that we would open a law office and continue working side by side. The state legislature had other plans. The state would not grant me a license to practice law because I was a woman.

4   My husband was not bothered by this turn of events. He had loved studying with me, but he was happy to provide for his family while I ran our home. I was devastated. I didn't have to go to college to be a homemaker. I spent my days **grieving** for the career I'd never have. I wished that I had never heard of the college, because then I'd be a happy wife. But then I wished something else. I wished that women could do anything we wanted to. I set out to find a way to change the law so we could.

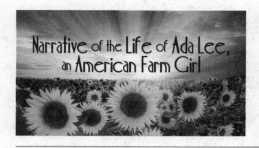

First Read

Read the story. After you read, answer the Think Questions below.

☁ **THINK QUESTIONS**

---

1. Where does Ada live in the beginning of the story? How do you know?

   Ada lives _____.

2. Write two or three sentences describing what happens when Ada goes to college.

   When Ada goes to college _____

   _____.

3. What problem(s) does Ada face at the end of the story? Cite textual evidence in your response.

   The problems Ada faces _____

   _____.

4. Use context clues to confirm the meaning of the word *earnest* as it is used in "Narrative of the Life of Ada Lee, an American Farm Girl." Write your definition of *earnest* here.

   Earnest means _____.

   A context clue is _____.

5. What is another way to say that a text is *incomprehensible*?

   A text is _____.

Please note that excerpts and passages in the StudySync® library and this workbook are intended as touchstones to generate interest in an author's work. The excerpts and passages do not substitute for the reading of entire texts, and StudySync® strongly recommends that students seek out and purchase the whole literary or informational work in order to experience it as the author intended. Links to online resellers are available in our digital library. In addition, complete works may be ordered through an authorized reseller by filling out and returning to StudySync® the order form enclosed in this workbook.

Reading & Writing Companion   151

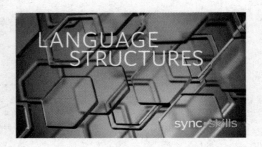

Skill:
Language Structures

★ DEFINE

In every language, there are rules that tell how to **structure** sentences. These rules define the correct order of words. In the English language, for example, a **basic** structure for sentences is subject, verb, and object. Some sentences have more **complicated** structures.

You will encounter both basic and complicated **language structures** in the classroom materials you read. Being familiar with language structures will help you better understand the text.

••• CHECKLIST FOR LANGUAGE STRUCTURES

To improve your comprehension of language structures, do the following:

✓ Monitor your understanding.

- Ask yourself: Why do I not understand this sentence? Is it because I do not understand some of the words? Or is it because I do not understand the way the words are ordered in the sentence?

✓ Pay attention to **perfect tenses** as you read. There are three perfect tenses in the English language: the present perfect, past perfect, and future perfect. The word *perfect* means "completed." These tenses describe actions that are completed or finished.

- **Present perfect tense** expresses an action that occurred at some indefinite time in the past.

> Combine *have* or *has* with the past participle of the main verb.

Example: I **have played** basketball for three years.

- **Past perfect tense** describes an action that happened before another action or event in the past.

> Combine *had* with the past participle of the main verb.

Example: I **had learned** how to dribble a ball before I could walk!

- **Future perfect tense** expresses one future action that will begin and end before another future event begins.

  > Use *will have* or *shall have* with the past participle of a verb.

  Example: Before the end of the year, I **will have played** more than 100 games!

✓ Break down the sentence into its parts.

- Ask yourself: What actions are expressed in this sentence? Are they completed or are they ongoing? What words give me clues about when an action is taking place?

✓ Confirm your understanding with a peer or teacher.

Please note that excerpts and passages in the StudySync® library and this workbook are intended as touchstones to generate interest in an author's work. The excerpts and passages do not substitute for the reading of entire texts, and StudySync® strongly recommends that students seek out and purchase the whole literary or informational work in order to experience it as the author intended. Links to online resellers are available in our digital library. In addition, complete works may be ordered through an authorized reseller by filling out and returning to StudySync® the order form enclosed in this workbook.

Reading & Writing Companion   **153**

YOUR TURN

Read the following excerpt from the text. Look at the bold-faced examples of past perfect tense. Remember that past perfect tense describes events that started and ended in the past. Then, sort the events into the order in which they happened. Place the correct letter in the chart below.

---

from **"Narrative of the Life of Ada Lee, an American Farm Girl"**

I sat down on the stool and dug my heels into the barn's dirt floor. "You know I love you, Bessie," I whispered dreamily to our dairy cow, "but I'm not going to be with you for much longer. I am going to college." A secret grin spread slowly across my face. It was the first time **I had said** my plan out loud. "I know what you're thinking, Bessie," I continued, patting her gently. Women could not go to college, but **I had heard** about a college on the east coast that would accept female students. The school was far away. The workload might be very hard, given my limited education. But I was determined to enroll. After all, **I had taught** myself to read. Learning from a teacher couldn't be harder than that. "It's going to be hard, but I will go to school and become a lawyer."

	Events
A	Ada teaches herself how to read.
B	Ada talks to Bessie about her plan to go to college.
C	Ada hears about a college that accepts female students.

First	Next	Last

Skill:
Comparing and Contrasting

★ DEFINE

To **compare** is to show how two or more pieces of information or literary elements in a text are similar. To **contrast** is to show how two or more pieces of information or literary elements in a text are different. By comparing and contrasting, you can better understand the **meaning** and the **purpose** of the text you are reading.

••• CHECKLIST FOR COMPARING AND CONTRASTING

In order to compare and contrast, do the following:

- ✓ Look for information or elements that you can compare and contrast.

    - Ask yourself: How are these two things similar? How are they different?

- ✓ Look for signal words that indicate a compare-and-contrast relationship.

    - Ask yourself: Are there any words that indicate the writer is trying to compare and contrast two or more things?

- ✓ Use a graphic organizer, such as a Venn diagram, to compare and contrast information.

Please note that excerpts and passages in the StudySync® library and this workbook are intended as touchstones to generate interest in an author's work. The excerpts and passages do not substitute for the reading of entire texts, and StudySync® strongly recommends that students seek out and purchase the whole literary or informational work in order to experience it as the author intended. Links to online resellers are available in our digital library. In addition, complete works may be ordered through an authorized reseller by filling out and returning to StudySync® the order form enclosed in this workbook.

Reading & Writing Companion   **155**

YOUR TURN

Read the following excerpt from the text. Then, complete the Compare-and-Contrast chart by writing the letter of the correct example in the chart below.

---

from "Narrative of the Life of Ada Lee, an American Farm Girl"

John and I worked together from then on. By the time we had earned our law degrees, we had grown quite close. We were married after graduation. It was my earnest wish that we would open a law office and continue working side by side. The state legislature had other plans. The state would not grant me a license to practice law because I was a woman.

My husband was not bothered by this turn of events. He had loved studying with me, but he was happy to provide for his family while I ran our home. I was devastated. I didn't have to go to college to be a homemaker. I spent my days grieving for the career I'd never have. I wished that I had never heard of the college, because then I'd be a happy wife. But then I wished something else. I wished that women could do anything we wanted to. I set out to find a way to change the law so we could.

	Examples
A	loved studying together in college
B	wasn't allowed to get a license
C	was allowed to get a license
D	wasn't bothered by the laws against women working
E	wanted to continue working together
F	was unhappy about not being able to have a career

Ada's Experience	Both	John's Experience

Close Read

 WRITE

PERSONAL RESPONSE: Think of a goal that you are trying to achieve. Are there any challenges? Is there anything stopping you? Write a short paragraph comparing and contrasting your experience to Ada Lee's story. Pay attention to main and helping verbs as you write.

Use the checklist below to guide you as you write.

☐ What is a goal you have?

☐ What problems do you have to face?

☐ How does your experience compare to Ada Lee's experiences?

☐ How does your experience contrast with Ada Lee's experiences?

Use the sentence frames to organize and write your personal response.

A goal I have is _____.

This goal is important to me because _____.

A problem I have is _____.

To solve the problem, I _____.

My experience is like Ada Lee's because _____.

Unlike Ada Lee, _____.

Please note that excerpts and passages in the StudySync® library and this workbook are intended as touchstones to generate interest in an author's work. The excerpts and passages do not substitute for the reading of entire texts, and StudySync® strongly recommends that students seek out and purchase the whole literary or informational work in order to experience it as the author intended. Links to online resellers are available in our digital library. In addition, complete works may be ordered through an authorized reseller by filling out and returning to StudySync® the order form enclosed in this workbook.

Reading & Writing Companion   **157**

PHOTO/IMAGE CREDITS:

cover, iStock.com/Figure8Photos
cover, ©iStock.com/eyewave, ©iStock.com/subjug, ©iStock.com/lvantsov, iStock.com/borchee, ©iStock.com/seb_ra
p. iv, iStock.com/anskuw
p. v, iStock.com/anskuw
p. v, iStock.com/antoni_halim
p. vi, iStock.com/anskuw
p. vi, iStock.com/DNY59
p. vi, iStock/fstop123/
p. vi, iStock/EHStock
p. vi, iStock/sdominick
p. vi, iStock/RapidEye
p. vii, iStock.com/hanibaram, iStock.com/seb_ra, iStock.com/Martin Barraud
p. vii, iStock.com/oonal
p. ix, iStock.com/Figure8Photos
p. x, Frederick Douglass - Archive Photos/Library of Congress/Stringer/Getty Images
p. x, Anya Groner - courtesy of Anya Groner
p. x, Frances Harper - Library of Congress/Contributor/Corbis Historical/Getty Images
p. x, Langston Hughes - Underwood Archives/Contributor/Archive Photos/Getty Images
p. x, Jack London - Chronicle/Alamy Stock Photo
p. xi, Thomas Ponce - courtesy of Thomas Ponce
p. xi, Ronald Reagan - IanDagnall Computing/Alamy Stock Photo
p. xi, Mahvash Sabet - Bahá'í International Community. www.bic.org
p. 0, iStock.com/
p. 1, Isle de Jean Charles Biloxi-Chitimacha-Choctaw Tribe
p. 2–14, Isle de Jean Charles Biloxi-Chitimacha-Choctaw Tribe
p. 20, iStock.com/
p. 21, ©iStock.com/GreenPimp
p. 22, ©iStock.com/GreenPimp
p. 23, ©iStock.com/Hohenhaus
p. 24, ©iStock.com/Hohenhaus
p. 25, iStock.com/
p. 26, Public Domain
p. 30, ©iStock.com/3DSculptor
p. 31, Bettmann/Bettmann/Getty Images
p. 33, ©iStock.com/3DSculptor
p. 34, ©iStock.com/
p. 35, ©iStock.com/
p. 36, ©iStock.com/Caval
p. 37, ©iStock.com/Caval
p. 38, ©iStock.com/3DSculptor
p. 39, iStock.com/MaggyMeyer
p. 40, ©2013 National Public Radio, Inc. NPR news report titled "A Kenyan Teen's Discovery: Let There Be Lights To Save Lions" by Nina Gregory as originally published on npr.org on March 1, 2013, and is used with the permission of NPR. Any unauthorized duplication is strictly prohibited.
p. 42, ©iStock.com/MaggyMeyer
p. 43, ©iStock.com/Hohenhaus
p. 44, ©iStock.com/Hohenhaus
p. 45, ©iStock.com/
p. 46, ©iStock.com/
p. 47, ©iStock.com/MaggyMeyer
p. 48, ©iStock.com/szefei
p. 51, ©iStock.com/kevron2001
p. 53, Library of Congress/Corbis Historical/Getty Images
p. 54, ©iStock.com/jaminwell
p. 58, Hulton Archive/Hulton Archive/Getty Images

p. 60, ©iStock.com/jaminwell
p. 61, ©iStock.com/eskaylim
p. 62, ©iStock.com/eskaylim
p. 63, ©iStock.com/fotogaby
p. 65, ©iStock.com/fotogaby
p. 66, ©iStock.com/jaminwell
p. 67, ©iStock.com/iLexx
p. 69, Steve Parsons - PA Images/PA Images/Getty Images
p. 71, ©iStock.com/iLexx
p. 72, ©iStock.com/donatas1205
p. 73, ©iStock.com/donatas1205
p. 74, ©iStock.com/Orla
p. 75, ©iStock.com/Orla
p. 76, ©iStock.com/iLexx
p. 77, ©iStock.com/KrivoTIFF
p. 78, Library of Congress/Corbis Historical/Getty Images
p. 80, ©iStock.com/KrivoTIFF
p. 81, ©iStock.com/
p. 82, ©iStock.com/
p. 83, ©iStock.com/Hohenhaus
p. 84, ©iStock.com/Hohenhaus
p. 85, ©iStock.com/KrivoTIFF
p. 86, Hendra Su/EyeEm/Getty
p. 88, Hendra Su/EyeEm/Getty
p. 89, ©iStock.com/Orla
p. 90, ©iStock.com/Orla
p. 91, Hendra Su/EyeEm/Getty
p. 92, ©iStock.com/hanibaram, iStock.com/seb_ra, iStock.com/Martin Barraud
p. 93, ©iStock.com/Martin Barraud
p. 99, ©iStock.com/gopixa
p. 102, ©iStock.com/ThomasVogel
p. 104, ©iStock.com/Tevarak
p. 107, ©iStock.com/Martin Barraud
p. 112, ©iStock.com/bo1982
p. 115, ©iStock/Jeff_Hu
p. 118, ©iStock.com/peepo
p. 121, ©iStock/Fodor90
p. 124, ©iStock.com/stevedangers
p. 127, ©iStock.com/Martin Barraud
p. 130, ©iStock.com/JStaley401
p. 132, iStock.com/
p. 134, iStock.com/
p. 136, ©iStock.com/Martin Barraud
p. 138, ©iStock.com/3DSculptor
p. 139, ©iStock.com/lolostock
p. 139, ©iStock.com/
p. 139, ©iStock.com/PeskyMonkey
p. 139, ©iStock.com/adventtr
p. 139, ©iStock.com/3DSculptor
p. 141, ©iStock.com/3DSculptor
p. 142, ©iStock.com/Ales_Utovko
p. 145, ©iStock.com/14951893
p. 147, ©iStock.com/3DSculptor
p. 148, ©iStock.com/Jag_cz
p. 149, ©iStock/Susan Chiang/
p. 149, ©iStock/Pamela Moore
p. 149, ©iStock/Wavebreak
p. 149, ©iStock/Christopher Futcher
p. 149, ©iStock.com/
p. 151, ©iStock.com/Jag_cz
p. 152, ©iStock.com/BlackJack3D
p. 155, ©iStock.com/RazvanDP
p. 157, ©iStock.com/Jag_cz

studysync

Text Fulfillment Through StudySync

If you are interested in specific titles, please fill out the form below and we will check availability through our partners.

ORDER DETAILS

Date:

TITLE	AUTHOR	Paperback/ Hardcover	Specific Edition *If Applicable*	Quantity

SHIPPING INFORMATION

Contact:

Title:

School/District:

Address Line 1:

Address Line 2:

Zip or Postal Code:

Phone:

Mobile:

Email:

BILLING INFORMATION ☐ SAME AS SHIPPING

Contact:

Title:

School/District:

Address Line 1:

Address Line 2:

Zip or Postal Code:

Phone:

Mobile:

Email:

PAYMENT INFORMATION

☐ CREDIT CARD

Name on Card:

Card Number: Expiration Date: Security Code:

☐ PO

Purchase Order Number:

StudySync Text Fulfillment, BookheadEd Learning, LLC
610 Daniel Young Drive | Sonoma, CA 95476